MW00365633

# The
# Compassion
# Fatigued
# Organization

Restoring Compassion to Helping Professionals

# The Compassion Fatigued Organization

## Restoring Compassion to Helping Professionals

### Michelle Graff

Cultivating
Human
Resiliency

Cultivating Human Resiliency, Kansas City, MO
resiliencyonline.com
© 2020 by Michelle Graff
All rights reserved

Editor: Shana Murph of Revise and Rewrite Editorial
Designer: Kelsey Klockenteger

ISBN-13 (print): 978-0-578-75315-7
ISBN-13 (e-book): 978-1-7358817-0-6

Library of Congress Preassigned Control Number: 2020918388

# Table of Contents

In memory of my mother, Shirley Graff, the first person to teach me about compassion.

—MG

# Introduction

A while back, I attended one of those trainings on burnout prevention. Everyone was asked to fill out a compassion fatigue screening and each person shared results. I scored high on stress and burnout and low on job satisfaction. This didn't surprise me at all, but I was a bit shocked by how many others in the class had scores that were as bad or worse than mine. In fact, all but one of us was suffering from compassion fatigue. She was a new hire, straight out of college.

The conversation became focused on her. People were saying things like, "You just wait until you've been doing this a while, you'll be just like the rest of us." We all took turns sharing horror stories about the things we'd seen and how the job had impacted us in not so good ways. It was almost as if we took pride in it. We wore our pain and callousness like some red badge of courage. On a break, I heard someone tell the poor girl, "You better learn to harden your heart, or it will eat you up."

That evening on my drive home, I started to think about it more. I had never really made the connection between my difficulty sleeping and stomach issues to my job. The worst part was what I had learned to do to survive this work had changed me. I had developed such a warped sense of humor and a negative way of looking at things that I called "realism," but it was not who I really was. When did I get like this? When I started my career, I had so much hope and purpose. When did I lose my compassion?

The place where I worked didn't help things either. Sure, they offered trainings on burnout and self-care. I guess that's better than nothing. But this was the same organization that demanded we carry an impossible caseload, always be on-call, and do not dare get behind. If something bad happened, it was our fault.

When management first started talking about self-care, we all thought it was a joke. When will we have time to do self-care? It felt like they were always setting us up to fail but it was our fault if we didn't take better care of ourselves.

It wasn't long after that training that I decided to leave the field all together. It took a long time after for the symptoms to go away. It still stresses me out to think back on those days. Kind of makes me sad that I lost the excitement I used to feel, thinking I was making a difference.

This story is one of many I have collected over the years in my work with human service organizations. I chose to open with it, not because it was the most extreme, but because it contained elements that I have heard repeatedly in conversations about compassion fatigue. To be honest, I see pieces of my own story in it.

The most tragic part of this story is that someone who was drawn to their work with people because of their compassion, felt they needed to leave the work to get it back. But what of the people that remain? What of the people who feel the need to "harden their hearts" just to survive the trenches of work that was intended to be compassionate? What toll do both these scenarios take on our communities?

This book was primarily written for the helping professionals, who labor to serve our community by providing service to those in need. But none of us work in isolation. We are impacted, not just by our exposure to secondary trauma, but also by the organizations and systems we work in.

Therefore, this book will examine the relationship between compassion-fatigued individuals and compassion-fatigued organizations, exploring the symptoms and causes of both. My intention is to go beyond raising awareness of the effects of secondary trauma on the human service industry. I hope to offer a path that builds resiliency and cultivates compassion.

If you are reading this introduction, you might be a health care worker, teacher, social worker, first responder or any of the many human service professionals serving our community. It does not matter if you are an executive leader, manager, or frontline professional. You are certain to identify some of the symptoms in you and your own organization. You will find that it will be easy to recognize your coworkers, employees or organizational leaders in the examples provided. Whoever you are, I would like to challenge you to read this book first as it applies to yourself and then think about how this applies to your organization. Doing so will not only deepen your understanding but prevent you from falling into a thinking pattern of blaming and helplessness.

I have provided both reflective and practice exercises to help in this self-application.

I am also going to challenge you to give yourself permission to be vulnerable. Recognize that your own responses are human and a reflection of human vulnerability, and at the same time, give yourself permission to see yourself as powerful. Regardless of your role, you are an agent of change that can shift the trajectory toward healing.

Finally, give yourself permission to be hopeful. Though the challenges facing the human service industry are great, look past the problems and toward the solutions. Together, we can make a difference.

Part I

# Why Is It So Dark in Here?

## Understanding Compassion Fatigue

Chapter 1

# Call for Action

I will begin with a humorous story that seemingly has nothing to do with human service, burnout, or compassion fatigue. Bear with me.

> Sally had just purchased a new home. It was a small older home in need of a makeover, but it was all hers. To celebrate, she invited her family and friends to a dinner party. As Sally worked to prepare the meal, small appliances buzzed in every outlet. Suddenly, silence and darkness swept the room.
>
> Oh no, thought Sally, what a terrible time to run out of power. Not knowing what else to do, Sally began to look around. To her delight, she discovered that the lights were still on in the dining room. Not to be deterred and pressed for time, she jumped into action. One by one, she moved each of the appliances to the dining room. With a short time remaining before her guests arrived, she got back to work.
>
> "Please, let me finish before the power runs out in this room too," she mumbled nervously to herself.

What does the plight of this young lady have to do with the compassion-fatigued organization, you might ask? In the story, our heroine finds a solution to a problem and continues toward her goal. Much like human service organizations, Sally demonstrates both motivation and a commitment to solve a problem. Unfortunately, her solution is only temporary because Sally does not realize that an overloaded circuit has tripped a breaker. The bigger problem still exists.

In my work with human service organizations, compassion fatigue is one of the most requested training or consultation topics. Most of my requests come from agencies that are already embarking on initiatives to create experiences that are more trauma informed for their clients. It is somewhat puzzling that the same organizations that recognize the need for their clients, struggle to apply these same principles to their employees and to themselves.

That is not to say there are no efforts in this area. I have seen a growing trend in organizations encouraging self-care. However, there is little evidence that this approach alone effectively mitigates the effects of secondary trauma exposure and compassion fatigue on organizations. At best, efforts lack a true understanding of what compassion fatigue is and how to best combat it, both individually and within the organizational culture.

## Why the struggle?

Since understanding compassion fatigue requires an understanding of trauma, I think it is helpful to examine some of the challenges human services have faced in becoming trauma informed.

Trauma theory is hardly new to the field of psychology. That is, it has long been theorized that traumatic experiences have a causal relationship with psychological distress. Why is it then that trauma-informed practices have taken so long to become the standard? The answer can be seen in a story about handwashing.

Did you know that the link between handwashing by physicians and lower mortality rates was first discovered in the 1840s? A physician named Ignaz Semmelweis oversaw a maternity clinic in Vienna. He noticed that the chance of a mother surviving delivery was not good. In fact, her chances were slightly worse in the maternity ward than delivering at home. Naturally, he began to wonder why. To test a hypothesis, he instructed the doctors to wash their hands in chlorine before tending to women in labor. The result was a mortality rate that dropped from one in ten to one in a hundred. He even published his findings. Yet it was almost fifty years later that handwashing became standard in the medical field and many years after that before this practice became common to the general public.

It seemed that the idea that sickness could be caused by something we could not see (germ theory was not introduced until decades later) was too large of a paradigm shift for the medical community to make, even in the face of hard evidence. For that shift to translate into practice took even longer.

Trauma theory requires a similar paradigm shift.

## History of trauma awareness

After the Vietnam War, leaders in behavioral health began to recognize symptoms that could be directly attributed to traumatic experiences. The term post-traumatic stress disorder (PTSD) became used to identify the effects of big trauma like combat exposure, mostly on adults.

It was not until 1998 that the Centers for Disease Control and Prevention and Kaiser Permanente released a study linking adverse childhood experiences (ACEs) to future psychological, social, and physical difficulties. This groundbreaking research gave way to a dramatic shift in the way we perceive and assist the people we serve. Instead of asking what is wrong with them, we ask what happened to them. This paradigm shift, however, has taken more than twenty years to comprehensively impact practice. One might argue that the social service, mental health, and education fields are still in the awareness stage of change.

If the human service industry is in the awareness stage regarding the effects of trauma on those we serve, we are only approaching this stage regarding the impact of trauma and secondary trauma on the industry and its organizations and workforce.

## Evolution of compassion fatigue awareness

The term compassion fatigue was introduced by Carla Joinson in her 1992 study of burnout in nursing. It is a condition affecting those who routinely care for others such as social workers, nurses, physicians, and first responders. It is the cumulative effect of chronic stress and exposure to the trauma of others, known as secondary or vicarious trauma.

Those who routinely witness the aftermath or hear stories of trauma can experience symptoms that mirror PTSD. Repeated exposure to secondary trauma is exacerbated by the chronic stress associated with the work. This leaves helping professionals feeling both mentally and physically exhausted. Those who suffer from compassion fatigue often report experiencing dissociative symptoms, such as being "in a fog." They can also struggle to feel empathetic toward clients. Additional symptoms can include distractibility, irritability, anxiety, and sleep disturbances as well as physical symptoms such as headaches and nausea.

In 1995, Charles Figley published *Compassion Fatigue: Secondary Traumatic Stress Disorders from Treating the Traumatized*. This drew more awareness to the problem and an interest in exploring approaches that mitigated the impact of compassion fatigue on individuals.

Still, the cumulative effects of secondary trauma and chronic stress continue to plague our human service organizations and helping professionals.

## What then?

Compassion fatigue is not just the problem of individuals. Human service organizations also suffer from chronic exposure to both primary and secondary trauma. Their organizational missions are impacted by not only the wellness of their workforce but by the wellness of the work culture. Ultimately, the service community suffers as well.

It seems imperative that effective strategies for combating compassion fatigue continue to be explored. This perhaps requires a deeper level of awareness to facilitate the difficult paradigm shift that, as helpers, we too require healing and compassion. In doing so, we must also examine approaches that recognize the need to build resiliency in compassion-fatigued organizations. Restoring compassion should be a number one priority.

In the case of Sally, imagine how different her response would have been if she only had a simple understanding of how houses were wired for electricity. Therefore, let us begin our journey of understanding compassion fatigue by examining the workings of the human brain.

Chapter 2
# The Brain

Although it is important to recognize the symptoms, understanding compassion fatigue begins with understanding the brain.

To know your brain is to embrace your humanity, and to acknowledge the humanity in others. The brain is a working model for all living organisms and relationships, including organizations and communities.

Technological advances have increased our scientific understanding of the human brain. But given that what we now know is only a fraction of what is yet to be discovered, we run the risk of overgeneralizing and oversimplifying this tremendously complex organ.

Most people recognize that the brain is made of many different regions performing different functions. Its complexity, however, lies in the way these regions work together through neuronal connections. Our complex nervous system has billions of pathways that send and receive messages across different regions of the brain and to the body.

For this book, we are going to focus on the functionality of this design. The brain has five important design elements that are important to the understanding of compassion fatigue.


## Design element one: The nature of the design, the brain is both physical and psychological

"Is it physical or is it just psychological?" This is a question that represents one of the many false dichotomies that are often believed about the human brain. There is an outdated notion that to treat a psychological problem, we must rule out a physical cause or vice versa. What neuroscience has shown us is that the two things are intertwined.

The term psychosomatic was coined to describe a physical problem that has an underlying psychological component. This does not mean that the problem is "all in your head." The truth is most inflictions have both a psychological and physical component. For example, obsessively worrying about the future could manifest physically, causing an ulcer or other chronic digestive problems. Conversely, chronic physical ailments can trigger psychological responses, such as depression. The brain plays a vital role in the functioning of all human systems, and the nervous system extends through the entire body. Symptoms of compassion fatigue manifest physically, emotionally, and cognitively.

## Design element two: Developmental drivers, this includes both nature and nurture

The age-old argument of nurture versus nature is probably not a dilemma at all. The answer is that it is both. Our DNA provides a blueprint for our development, but our experiences influence how that developmental map is followed. The brain is constantly wiring and rewiring itself to adapt to its environment.

For example, you might have inherited a predisposition for reading competency from your parents, however, how often they read to you during your early childhood will influence how this competency is developed. Another example is the degree to which you are introverted. Though there is some genetic influence on this personality trait, if you are raised in an unsafe environment, you might adapt to this environment by turning inward. Conversely, if you experience a safe environment with support and encouragement, you might have the opportunity to develop some extroverted traits.

So past experiences not only drive future responses, they impact the physical makeup of our brain. This may sound fatalistic, but fortunately, the brain's plasticity also allows for positive experiences that create opportunities for growth and healing.

## Design element three: Developmental goals, this includes both to survive and to thrive

When we experience a threat that we lack the resources to cope with, our brain kicks into survival mode and activates a flight, fight, or freeze response.

The responses of flight, fight, and freeze are our built-in protective mechanisms that are triggered automatically when we detect a threat. In a literal sense, if you encounter a predator, your survival response would be to injure or scare the predator off (fight), run away (flight), or stay completely still and hope you go unnoticed (freeze.) Threats are perception based, and fight, flight, and freeze responses are not always so literal. A more relatable scenario might be your boss demanding you do something that you are afraid to do. Your survival responses could include yelling at your boss (fight), making excuses to avoid responsibility (flight), or not responding at all and hoping your boss forgets he asked (freeze).

Experiencing a threat that triggers a survival response not only strengthens these response pathways, but it shapes the way our brain will perceive or interpret future experiences and stimuli. This is what trauma reenactment is. A current emotion or stressful situation is interpreted as a threat based on past experiences and so triggers a patterned survival response.

Yet the brain is not designed for survival alone, it is also designed to thrive. We can learn and apply our learning to new situations. Growth and healing involve distinguishing the past from the present and finding ways to create a new response.

## Design element four: Interpretive functions, this includes both perceptions and emotions

The brain is constantly mining data and searching for patterns that create a worldview to assist in interpreting reality and to allow us to both survive and thrive.

Our perceptions formed by past experiences are designed to be helpful navigational tools that assist in learning and maintaining safety. It can also be misleading. This was demonstrated a few years ago when a photograph of a dress went viral, causing a heated debate about whether it was white and gold or blue and black. More than half of the people viewing the photo perceived it as white and gold, while many disagreed vehemently. In short, the difference in perception has to do with how our brain interprets light and shadow. The brain "autocorrects" visual data based on what it has learned about how light changes color. The truth is that the dress was blue and black. The reality is that not everyone's brain interpreted the photo the same way.

This process applies to much more than just visual data. Among other things, it is how we learn about language, safety, relationships, and our sense of self in relation to the rest of the world.

Another interpretive function of the brain is our emotions. Our brain uses emotions to encode memories so that we can better identify future threats. Equally, positive emotions are associated with pleasurable activities that are more likely to lead us to life sustaining responses. Though, like perceptions, emotions can lead to misinterpretations.

## Design element five: Role of relationships, they serve to both nurture and protect

From our first breath outside our mother's womb, we are instinctively aware of our need for relationships. We are wired to connect. This connection is essential for survival. Human infants are unable to care for themselves and remain that way longer than any other mammal. But in addition to our need to survive, relationships are at the core of all learning and healthy growth and development. Our caregivers are the first windows to the world around us and parent-child interactions begin to shape the way the child perceives his environment.

This dependency goes beyond infancy. Our ancestors needed the protection of the clan, just as a newborn is totally dependent on others for survival. Even though today we live in a culture that promotes independence, human beings are by nature interdependent.

In our roles as helping professionals, we continually engage in relationships that lack reciprocity. This is by design. However, we cannot deny the inevitable toll it takes on human beings who are wired to connect and receive safety through relationships.

All five of these design elements offer insight into how people exposed to secondary trauma develop compassion fatigue. But they also hold the key to understanding possible solutions.

# Chapter 3

# Secondary Trauma and Compassion Fatigue

## What is compassion fatigue?

As stated earlier, compassion fatigue impacts those in helping professions, such as nurses, physicians, first responders, therapists, social workers, teachers, and other professionals, who work with people who have experienced trauma. Exposure to secondary trauma can involve witnessing the events, the aftermath, or the effects of the trauma on the person. It can also involve reading or hearing the stories of trauma victims.

The circuit breaker box in my home provides a good analogy to help us understand compassion fatigue. Like Sally, we have probably all had the experience of having too many electrical appliances running at once. As a safety feature, this circumstance can sometimes "trip the breaker." When this happens, the power goes out. To someone who does not understand how a house is wired or what a circuit breaker is, it probably would seem like the house lost power when the breaker is tripped. The truth is the electricity has not been depleted. We just need to unplug a few things and reset the circuit breaker to restore power.

Compassion fatigue is our survival response to chronic stress and exposure to the pain and trauma of others. When our amygdala senses a threat, it sends the signal that a protective response is needed. It "trips the breaker" as part of our brain's built-in safety feature. Like when our home seems to be "out of power," symptoms of compassion fatigue include feeling depleted of compassion. This sensation and other symptoms can be better understood by examining how the brain and body responds to threats.

Our autonomic nervous system controls unconscious body functions, such as breathing, heart rate, circulation, and digestion. It is made up of two opposing systems. When the parasympathetic side of the autonomic nervous system is stimulated, it helps to regulate our normal body functions. But when the brain sends the distress signal, the sympathetic side prepares the body for fight or flight by increasing heart rate, concentrating blood flow, and slowing down the body functions it determines to be less essential.

In addition to stimulating the "fight or flight" responses of the sympathetic nervous system, the brain can also trigger a "freeze" survival response. This can include the numbing of emotions and avoiding empathetic responses that leave us vulnerable to more pain. Helping professionals can be constantly triggered into this freeze response by repeat exposure to secondary trauma. This can lead them to believe that they are depleted of compassion, as it is often described.

In fact, this is not the case. Compassion is renewable. But, too often, helping professionals do not take the time or are unaware of the need to reset.

## Recognizing the symptoms

Not surprisingly, the symptoms of chronic exposure to secondary trauma mirror symptoms of primary trauma. Though the perceived threat differs, the response is similar. In the case of compassion fatigue, the threat becomes the compassionate work we do. When our brains interpret an action as a threat, our body is triggered to fight, flight, or freeze. These responses manifest as physical, emotional, and cognitive symptoms. Sufferers of compassion fatigue can experience symptoms of arousal triggered by our fight and flight responses as well as symptoms of avoidance through a freeze response.

Cognitively, arousal responses can include extreme or negative thinking, intrusive thoughts, increased cynicism, disturbing dreams, and rumination. Avoidant cognitive responses include minimizing the pain of others, difficulty focusing, impaired decision making and dissociation.

Emotionally, arousal responses can include irritability, anger, irrational fears, and experiences of emotional overload. Emotional avoidance includes numbing, depression, dread of work, diminished enjoyment, and detachment.

Physical symptoms of arousal include sleeplessness, headaches, and digestive problems, including loss of appetite. Physical freeze responses include diminished energy, immobility, and exhaustion.

> **Reflective Exercise:** Since helping professionals have different experiences and coping resources, their symptoms will also vary. Use the symptom chart provided at the end of this chapter to identify your own experience with compassion fatigue or what you have seen in your organization. This list is not all-inclusive. You may identify symptoms that fall into the categories that are not already mentioned.

Ironically, the qualities that draw people to choose a helping profession can also make them more vulnerable to suffering from the symptoms of compassion fatigue. For example, the ability to be empathetic allows us to feel another's suffering. This is something the brain can interpret as a threat. The helping professional's history of trauma can increase this vulnerability. Past experiences can shape what triggers a flight, fight, and freeze response. Other contributing factors include those working with the young or extremely vulnerable, as well as work that sees limited success or progress. All these vulnerabilities have something in common. They impact either what the brain identifies as a threat or its perceived ability to control or mitigate that threat.

## The antidote

The great paradox of compassion fatigue is that compassion is not only the trigger, it is the antidote. We do not need less compassion; we need to restore its ability to heal and connect us.

It is an inevitable truth that we cannot deny compassion for others without denying compassion for ourselves and we cannot withhold self-compassion without eventually withholding it from others. Therefore, combating compassion fatigue and restoring compassion is crucial for both helping professionals and human service organizations.

There are two important components of compassion. The first involves being attuned to the suffering of others. The second involves being motivated to respond in a way that alleviates the other's pain. Compassionate responses can include offering an empathetic presence such as listening without judgment, communicating you care, or just sitting with someone who is suffering. It can also include an intervening action such as offering direct assistance or contributing to causes that benefit others.

There is a growing body of research supporting the idea that compassion can have a positive effect on the compassion giver as well as the recipient. A compassionate response has been shown to both calm the threat response while triggering the reward system. Though the brain still detects the suffering, which triggers a distress signal in the insula region of the brain, our prefrontal cortex begins to develop a plan. This calms the amygdala. When we have enough resources to cope with a situation, it is no longer interpreted as a threat. Instead, acts of compassion can trigger our reward system causing dopamine pathways to fire. Additionally, the neurochemical oxytocin, which promotes overall well-being, is triggered by the distress signal but also produced when we respond with a prosocial interaction.

The likelihood that we choose a compassionate response to assist another versus a protective response to withdraw from the pain can be increased with practice. Cultivating compassion can be compared to exercising a muscle. When we exercise our ability to respond compassionately, we increase our ability to focus on suffering without distress.

The ability to face our fears and turn toward the suffering of others instead of away can be cultivated. It begins with self-awareness and self-regulation, and it involves shifting our mindsets, identifying emotional triggers, and using regulation to expand our range of tolerance. It also involves an ongoing commitment to practice skills that strengthen our ability to choose compassionate responses.

Similarly, to combat organizational compassion fatigue, we must cultivate a culture of compassion. This involves skill sets and mindsets that go beyond encouraging self-care. Though self-care is a component of addressing exposure to secondary trauma, it is only one piece of the pie. Cultivating compassion involves a comprehensive and deliberate shift in our cognitive, emotional, and behavioral responses. In individuals, these skills involve practice until they become habit. Cultivating compassion in organizations involves embedding these practices in the culture.

# Symptoms of Compassion Fatigue

## Cognitive

Increased cynicism
Intrusive repetitive thoughts
Extreme/negative thinking
Intrusive dreams/nightmares

Difficulty focusing
Impaired decision-making
Minimizing others' pain
Dissociation

## Emotional

Irritability
Anger
Anxiety
Irrational fears
Despair

Depression
Dread of work
Diminished enjoyment
Numbing
Detachment

## Physical

Sleeplessness
Headaches
Digestive problems

Diminished energy
Immobility
Exhaustion

Part II

# Getting the Lights Back On:

Self-Awareness and Regulation

Sally's story could be my story. I too tripped a circuit breaker while preparing a dinner party in my first home. The difference being that I knew what a circuit breaker was. However, since it was a new home, I was not at all familiar with that breaker box. After eventually locating the box in the basement, I discovered it was not labeled. So it took a while to figure out which circuit I needed to reset.

Just as it was important for me to learn my way around my own house, it is important for helping professionals and human service organizations to be aware of their own triggers and response patterns.

I am often asked to provide training on burnout prevention, stress management, or even self-care by organizations struggling with low morale and high turnover. Many of these agencies are in the process of becoming trauma informed. The stories sound familiar: An organization commits to becoming more trauma informed, trains its staff, implements trauma-informed approaches or treatment techniques but still struggles with some of the same old problems.

Becoming trauma informed involves shifting our thinking about those we serve from "What's wrong with you?" to "What happened to you?" So most agencies begin by training frontline staff on the effects of trauma on their clients.

This training is an important step in becoming trauma informed. However, if we were to go back to our circuit breaker analogy, focusing only on our client's trauma is like solving the problem of a tripped breaker by examining the toaster.

To understand the effects of trauma, we need to understand our own triggers and responses and ability to self-regulate. Instead of beginning with clients or frontline staff, when I work with an organization, I like to start with the leadership team. When they can recognize their triggers; when they recognize how their response patterns contribute or detract from a trauma-informed culture; when they practice self-regulation, real change begins. That is not to say that change needs to come from the top down, as this is often not the case. Change does, however, need to come from within.

In a sense, to be effective in human service, we need to first embrace our own humanity so we can see the humanity in others.

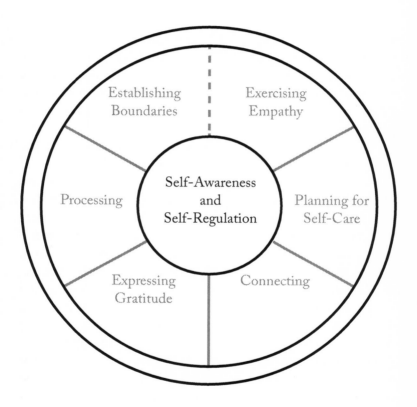

# Chapter 4

# Body Response

Awareness of our thoughts and emotions help us to understand what and why situations are interpreted by our brain as threatening. This gives us insight into our survival triggers. But, from a hierarchical view of the nervous system, understanding survival response begins with awareness of our physiological response. When we learn how to listen to our body, we are better able to recognize when we have been triggered.

To understand how our body responds to these triggers, we need to reexamine our autonomic nervous system.

Our nervous system includes somatic and autonomic responses. Our autonomic response system involves those responses that are outside our control or awareness. These systems of nerves connect with the other anatomical systems, such as the respiratory, circulatory, and digestive systems, that regulate important body functions.

The autonomic nervous system is divided into two parts, the sympathetic and the parasympathetic. These two systems are opposing in that when one is triggered, the other is dormant. Both nervous systems affect organs, glands, muscles, and systems throughout our body. The sympathetic system of nerves stems from the spinal cord, whereas the parasympathetic originates at both the brain stem and near the digestive tract. However, the main difference between these two systems is the response messages they relay.

The sympathetic response is a response of mobility. It is designed to ready our body for action. This response is often characterized as flight or fight responses. When this system is triggered, our pupils become dilated, our breathing increases, and our heart rate becomes more rapid. Blood circulation is concentrated on larger muscles to increase our ability to mobilize to defend. Areas that the brain deems as less necessary, like our digestive functions, are inhibited.

This inhibition to the digestive system can contribute to the digestive problems experienced by some helping professions suffering from compassion fatigue.

The parasympathetic response is a response of homeostasis. It is responsible for regulating all systems necessary to maintain good health. When this system is triggered, the body returns to its normal functioning. The heart rate lowers, with circulation returning to all areas of the body. This allows fine motor functioning and cognitive abilities to be restored. Breathing slows and becomes steadier. Less critical but necessary functions are restored. The parasympathetic nervous system is sometimes characterized as the rest and digest response, because it returns the body to its resting state and restores regular digestion.

Regulation is often seen as the ability to trigger our parasympathetic response system and return to homeostasis. However, remember that fight and flight are only part of our survival response. The Polyvagal theory, proposed by neuroscientist Stephen Porges, suggests that the parasympathetic response can also be divided into two response pathways. The ventral vagal (vagus being the primary nerve of the parasympathetic system) is the response of regulation and social engagement. The dorsal vagal pathway, the more evolutionarily primitive response, is that of freeze. In this response system, the body begins to disengage and shut down. This response is triggered when the sympathetic nervous system becomes too aroused or in threatening situations that are too overwhelming. Think of it as an overcorrection by our parasympathetic nervous system.

It is important not to malign our all-too-human sympathetic nervous system responses. I find it helpful to think of regulation as a continuum between mobility and immobility. Though the sympathetic nervous system is activated when triggered by toxic stress and perceived threats, it also serves as a necessary function in our everyday lives. While it was never designed to be activated all the time, we also were not designed to be constantly at rest. We need to be mobilized to get things accomplished. Most importantly, it is our sympathetic nervous system that is activated in moments of love and courage.

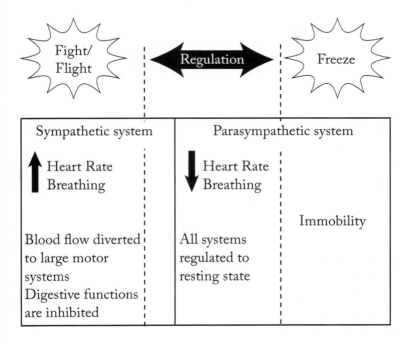

Though fight, flight, and freeze responses occur not just in our autonomic nervous system, awareness of our body responses can help us identify when we need self-regulation. As stated earlier, our bodies were not designed to be held in threat-response mode. Helping professionals that experience continuous exposure to stress and trauma can begin to suffer chronic physical symptoms. Organizations suffer the results of having a workforce that has been physically compromised and exhausted. Without the ability to recognize and reset, this trajectory ultimately impairs the work we set out to accomplish.

# Chapter 5

# Emotional Response

Survival responses, fight, flight, and freeze are more than just physical occurrences. These triggered responses can also occur in our emotions. In fact, feelings can be described as both physical and emotional responses. It is sometimes difficult to distinguish the two, as they often go hand in hand. To better understand the emotional aspect of the survival response, let us explore the function of emotions.

Being emotional in our culture can have a negative connotation and has often been synonymous with weakness or the absence of logic. The truth is that emotions are a necessary function of the human brain. To be emotional is to be human. They serve an interpreter role and play a key part in decision-making. As to whether it helps or hinders our ability to make sound decisions, well, that depends. Like our thoughts, emotions can be misinterpreted or cause us to misread a situation. Though, primarily they are there to help.

Emotional responses such as fear and happiness are temporary states produced in our brain, shaped by our memories and perceptions. When we experience an event that is converted into long-term memory, the brain tags the memory with an emotion to help us later discern if future situations are safe or life threatening. Like other feelings such as hunger or pain, they guide our responses and help us to navigate life.

Emotions themselves are not right or wrong, but sometimes they are based on an inaccurate or outdated perception.

I like to think of emotion as being like the GPS navigational systems we use in our cars. With a strong signal and a good mapping program, it can provide our location and directional assistance to help us get where we want to go. However, any navigational system is only as good as the data it was programmed with and its ability to connect to the GP satellites. If you have ever experienced using a GPS that is operating on an old program or a weak signal, you know that they can lead you to make wrong turns.

Our brain has its own navigational system. The basic program we are born with is wired for survival to help us respond to threats and guide us to life-sustaining actions. Our brain uses new data gained through life experiences to expand and adapt this programming. It is constantly rewiring and forming new neuronal pathways. When we feel an emotion, it is a signal giving us information about our current state. It is necessary to stay attuned to our present emotional states. Though, like any navigational system, distorted perceptions based on outdated or inaccurate information can cause our initial emotional response to be unreliable.

**Reflective Exercise:** The day in and day out decisions of helping professionals can be impaired by emotions. This is especially true when the emotion has triggered us into a survival mode, causing reactive decisions. Just like the advice, "Never make a permanent decision based on a temporary emotion," a more effective decision-making device is to practice value-based decisions.

Values are the core principles and beliefs that we hold dear. Values have an emotional component but require greater deliberation. Because they are shaped and developed throughout our lifetime, they can offer more truth and stability than a fleeting emotion. In the navigation system analogy, values are more like the compass that reliably points north. It provides both consistent and accurate information on where we are and which direction we need to be headed.

Whether it is an individual decision or an organizational decision, here are some helpful questions to make sure it is value based:

- **What is the prevailing emotion?** Begin by acknowledging the emotion without judgment. Remember that emotions themselves are not right or wrong; they are a necessary part of being human.
- **What outdated perceptions might be influencing my current emotional state?** Examining our perceptions can help us root out negative or inaccurate thoughts that keep us stuck in unhelpful response patterns.
- **What are my top three core values?** Prioritizing what is most important to us helps ensure we are acting in ways that guide us in the direction we want to go.
- **What are the guiding principles to which I need to adhere?** Both professionally and personally, it is helpful to have a standard set of precepts that remain the same, regardless of our current situation.
- **What is the response that best reflects these values and principles?** We are what we do. Decisions based on what you deeply value will always get you closer to your true goals than ones based on immediate relief or reward.

## Emotional triggers

To better understand emotional triggers, let us take a closer look at the amygdala. The amygdala is an almond-shaped part of the brain in our limbic system. It is responsible for the quick responses to strong emotions and threats. It is the amygdala that sets off our survival responses of flight, fight, and freeze. It should be noted that the amygdala also plays a role in the brain's pleasure response system.

In times of a real threat, the amygdala responds quickly to keep us safe from harm. So the amygdala serves an important and necessary function. Unfortunately, when we have experienced past trauma or chronic adversity, our brain starts to generalize. Situations that are not in reality a threat can begin to produce strong emotions and trigger survival responses. This happens so quickly that we are usually not even consciously aware of it. Remember, it is not just the situation that triggers the response. It is also the strong emotion.

So memory is encoded with emotions to help our survival brain to identify threats and to determine what causes pleasure and what causes pain. However, we know that the complex brain is not just built for survival, and humans experience many more emotional nuances than just pleasure and pain. Though when in survival mode, the brain generalizes, and many emotions can be interpreted as threats. Fear, shame, worry, and envy are just some examples of emotions that can signal a threat response.

To fully understand why our brain can interpret these emotions as threats we need to examine human needs. In their Self-Determination Theory, Deci and Ryan identified autonomy, relatedness, and competency as basic psychological needs that drive human motivation. Remember, to survive in this world we either need to control external threats or manage them with our external or internal resources. This requires that we be either extremely competent, or we belong to a community to protect us, or we have complete control over our environment.

Though it is not difficult to understand why fear produces a threat response since it is often linked directly to perceived danger, let us examine how other emotions can be interpreted as threats.

## Shame

First let us distinguish shame from guilt. Guilt is the feeling that occurs when we do something that is in contradiction with our personal values or of the morals of society. Guilt is an emotion that can motivate us to make amends or change our behavior in positive ways. The difference between guilt and shame is that guilt tells us that we did something wrong, shame tells us that there is something wrong with us.

Shame sometimes goes unidentified because, at a cognitive level, people might understand their worth. However, someone can have good self-esteem and still feel shame. Because the opposite of shame is not self-esteem; the opposite of shame is belonging. Since belonging is an essential need of every human, shame is a universal human feeling.

Experiences and messages that contradict our sense of relationship and belongingness can shake our sense of worth, regardless of self-esteem. Shame is believing you are unworthy of belonging. This is the reason rejection evokes such painful feelings for most people. Shame can also be a form of rejection we impose on ourselves. By accepting our wrongness, we are rejecting our place in humanity.

Helping professionals that engage in client relationships that by nature are not reciprocated can constantly trigger feelings of shame. Circumstances provoking a sense of not doing enough or letting people down are also common.

## Envy

Envy is rooted in both our need to belong and our need to be competent. Our need to belong causes us to look to others for comparison to see how we measure up. As we will further explore in the next chapter, scarcity and polarized thinking contribute to a distorted belief that all is measured on opposing scales. This can lead to a mindset that when someone else has something, be it an admired characteristic or possession, it means we are somehow less. Feelings of envy then can be interpreted as a threat to both our competence and our belonging.

For helping professionals, this emotion cannot only be interpreted as threat, but it can rob them of the joy they used to get from seeing others do well.

# Worry

Worry occurs when we fear an outcome we cannot control. Therefore, it is also a threat to both our sense of competency and control. Helping professionals work in environments where the stakes are high. Often negative outcomes can be tragic, and positive outcomes are minimal with many factors beyond the control of the helping professional.

When strong emotions are triggered, we respond in ways that attempt to restore our sense of control, competency, and belonging.

## Emotions as responses

When regulated, emotions are a normal part of human functioning. They are present whether we are cognitively aware of them or not. In our thrive mode, both positive and negative emotions have varying nuances and complexity. Indeed, the list of emotional words in our language is vast. We are also capable of experiencing more than one emotion at a time.

However, in survival mode, they take on a fight, flight, or freeze response, and the list can narrow to anger, anxiety, and depression.

## Fight

When a situation threatens our sense of control, often the emotional response of anger can be provoked. Anger is an emotional response that usually masks other more vulnerable emotions. Emotionally, anger prepares us for the fight.

## Flight

An emotional flight response is an attempt to escape threat or emotional discomfort. Anxiety can be the emotional response in preparation for mobilizing away from the threat.

## Freeze

When emotions become too overwhelming, a freeze response is triggered, allowing us to numb our emotions. After all, sayings like "died of a broken heart," or "scared to death," came into our language for a reason. Emotions are powerful and sometimes dangerous.

Unfortunately, emotions cannot be numbed selectively. An emotional freeze response usually results in the dulling of other emotional experiences. Over time, this numbing can become associated with what is referred to as depression. Though the term "depressed" is most often associated with sadness, depression is more than just a specific emotion. It diminishes the ability to feel all emotions, including positive ones. One can experience sadness without being in a state of depression, just as one can be sad and experience other emotions at the same time.

The emotional responses of anger, anxiety, and depression can each be perceived by the survival brain as one individual emotion. However, all three are emotion clusters with associated cognitive and physical reactions. For example, anxiety can involve many emotional nuances, such fear, worry, and nervousness as well as cognitive and physical symptoms, such as persistent thoughts and nausea. Just as anger can be a combination of frustration, shame, humiliation, or disappointment, and might be accompanied by other symptoms, such as negative thinking and muscle tension.

It is also true that people who struggle with anger or anxiety or depression often struggle with one or more of the other two as well, because all three are survival responses.

## Emotional awareness

In teaching emotional management to children, we often use the language that emotions can be too big. This is when they become overwhelming and difficult to manage. They can also become too small. When this happens, we are unable to detect them or deal with them. This language can also be helpful for adults. We need to be aware of our emotions before we can develop the skill set necessary to tolerate them.

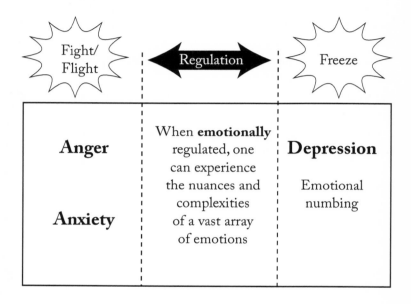

In the name of "emotional management," some mistakenly believe that they are controlling their emotions by not expressing them. Emotions are meant to be felt, not avoided. Avoided emotions tend to resurface in the form of unhelpful responses. If our emotions cause us to respond in ways contrary to our values or in ways that are destructive to ourselves and our relationships, they are controlling us.

In fact, to effectively deal with emotions, we must first *feel it to face it.*

In doing so, it helps to remember two basic truths about emotions:

- They are a characteristic of being human.
- They are temporary.

It might also be helpful to remember that emotions come from our thoughts, memories, perceptions, and beliefs. Emotions are real, but when they are rooted in the past, they can be shaped by an old perception or belief that may or may not be accurate.

Emotional intelligence, which includes emotional awareness and the ability to manage interpersonal responses, is gaining recognition as a necessary leadership skill. However, organizations often do little to encourage the practice of *feel it to face it*. Often, remnants remain in organizational culture that diminish the value of emotion identification. When explicit and implicit messages indicate that emotions are still seen as weak rather than human, underlying emotions go unaddressed, allowing them to continue to drive organizational reactivity.

# Chapter 6

# Cognitive Responses

Fight, flight, and freeze responses occur cognitively just as they do physically and emotionally. Cognitively, the brain's freeze response is denial or dissociation. The fight or flight response is cognitive defensiveness. When in survival mode, our brain distorts information to facilitate a protective response. Unfortunately, these distortions exacerbate our cognitive defensiveness. Self-awareness involves knowing our brain and recognizing our vulnerability to get stuck in the trappings of our own mind. These vulnerabilities make us more susceptible to the cognitive symptoms of compassion fatigue.

| Fight/Flight | ←— Regulation —→ | Freeze |
|---|---|---|
| **Defensiveness**<br><br>**Distortion** | When **cognitively** regulated, the opportunity for learning, innovation, and complex thinking is heightened | **Denial**<br><br>**Dissociation** |

# Mind traps

The idea that our brain takes shortcuts that can lead us to faulty thinking is not a product of modern neuroscience. Philosophers and logic professors have recognized fallacies or thinking errors for centuries. But new discoveries of just how our brain works leads to new insights into why our brain so often tricks us.

Do not get me wrong; the brain is not just an unreliable trickster. It is incredibly designed to both survive and to thrive (that is, to learn, grow, and heal). It functions in ways to achieve these goals within the world we live.

Surviving the world would be easy if we were all-knowing and could rapidly process every bit of data available in any given moment. Though, be careful what you wish for. It is possible this level of awareness might keep us from enjoying and appreciating the beauty of life. At least, I think it would make it difficult to get a good night's sleep. So the brain finds clever ways to achieve its goals with the information it has available.

First, when registering an interpretation of incoming data, the brain uses what it has previously learned. In fact, for adults, there are more neurotransmissions being sent from within the brain than there is new information provided by the external experience. In other words, our interpretation of any given reality might be based more on what we already think we know than what we are actually experiencing.

Secondly, the brain does not like ambiguity. Our survival mode brain knows that what you do not know can hurt you. In the absence of data, it tends to fill in the gap. This can lead us to jump to conclusions or overinterpret meaning or cause and effect relationships.

The ability to selectively pay attention to what is important and fill in the gaps for everything else can lead to distortions that can result in mind traps. Before identifying common mind traps, I want to review the interpretation of data through the processes of generalization and assimilation.

We know that experiences help us to learn and grow. From our first moments of life, our brains are searching for patterns that allow us to make sense of the world. The data is stored as memory for later use. To add efficiency to this process, the brain generalizes what it learns. This enables us to learn and adapt more quickly. For example, a person touches a candle and gets burned. He probably does not need to stick his hand in every open flame to see if it, too, is going to burn. Our brain will generalize the information about the candle to all other flames.

Both positive and negative experiences develop our worldview or our working model of how we perceive the world to be. New experiences will be interpreted through the lens of this working model. We call this assimilation. The brain does this much more than we are aware of and forms a perception of the world that becomes as much rooted in our past experiences as it is reality.

Though it is possible for new experiences to challenge and reshape our worldview, after a certain age, it becomes easier to assimilate the new experience into what we already believe. This feature of our brain leads to something often referred to as confirmation bias. That is the tendency to use new information to support what we already believe and reject information that challenges our belief, regardless of the weight, validity, or content of the new data.

So the natural processes of generalization and assimilation help the brain achieve the thrive goal of learning and growing. However, if triggered in survival mode, the brain uses these functions to stay safe in four ways that can alter our perception of the world.

## The survival brain tries to simplify the complex, resulting in a polarized view of reality.

When our primary goal becomes safety, the brain does not need to be distracted with complexity. Therefore, it simplifies things by narrowing the categories of identification. No time for nuances; everything is either this or that. This polarized view helps the brain make quick, and sometimes lifesaving decisions.

Expressions like "do or die" and "kill or be killed" are a representation of this mentality.

Polarized thinking produces such mind traps as the false dilemma, seeing only two choices when there is a continuum of possibilities.

*"That situation is not as dire as those I work with, so it doesn't deserve my sympathy."*

Another mind trap caused by polarized thinking is the false dichotomy. This is when we perceive that something must be one or the other, when both possibilities can exist.

*"I can either take care of myself or take care of others."*

A common example of a false dichotomy is the idea that people are either rational or emotional. This polarized view sets up a negative stigmatization associated with being emotional. In turn, both emotional expression and validation become discouraged. The reality is, it is not an all-or-nothing proposition. The ability to be both rational and emotional is part of what makes us human.

Polarized thinking can be seen in our view of those we serve as being so different from ourselves. Ironically, this way of thinking can sometimes be perpetuated in the trauma-informed movement.

The old model of thinking was that there was a stark difference between care workers and care recipients. What separated professionals from their clients was their clients' problems or whatever was identified as wrong with them. This prevailing mindset undermined the shared humanity of both. The trauma-informed movement rightly shifted the focus from what was wrong with people to what happened to them. With that mindset, the only thing separating the professional from the client was his or her trauma. However, there still exists an underlying belief that there are those who are traumatized and those who help them. This too is a myth. Trauma experiences are universally human and professionals, who are continuously exposed to the trauma of others, suffer the same effects. Thus, exposing an uncomfortable reality that the only thing separating the helping professional from the service recipient is nothing. Both individual and organizational responses are often implicitly designed to avoid or deny this reality.

This distorted thinking can cause the helping professional to minimize their own experiences with trauma and ignore the resulting signs of distress.

Organizations reinforce this distorted perception by minimizing or ignoring the impact of secondary trauma and responding punitively to the workers' symptoms of distress.

## The survival brain conserves resources resulting in the perception as finite, that which is replenishable.

When threatened, the brain performs a sort of mental triage so that all available resources can be focused on the primary goal of survival. When the survival brain conducts this inventory of resources, it is only focused on what is available in the here and now. It, therefore, assumes that all resources are finite. Over time, this can lead to a mind trap of scarcity thinking.

When we are exposed to chronic stress and secondary trauma, this can mean that anything not classified as critical enough does not warrant our attention.

Additionally, past experiences of perceived deprivation reinforce scarcity thinking and can distort our view of what we need, want, and deserve and how we measure fairness.

Scarcity thinking, in combination with polarized thinking can result in a distorted sense of fairness in which everything is

56

measured on opposing scales. If someone has something it must be to the exclusion of someone else. This view is often applied to the intangible and the replenishable, such as love, affirmation, mercy, and compassion.

When compassion is viewed as a finite resource, we run the risk of perceiving it as something that needs to be conserved rather than shared generously.

## The survival brain slows down the perception of time, resulting in a diminished capacity to distinguish past, present, and future.

Time is a tricky thing to wrap our minds around because of its perpetual nature. We all experience time in past, present and future, but the present is temporary and fleeting. In survival mode, our perception of time slows down. This phenomenon is attributed to our brain hyper-recording sensory information when it detects danger. This perception can cause us to attribute too much weight to past experiences, especially if they are encoded with strong emotion. What happened in the past can feel very much as if it is occurring in the present. Additionally, we can easily forget the temporariness of the present. When things are unpleasant, it feels like it lasts forever.

An overemphasis of the past can interfere with our ability to imagine the future, resulting in a diminished sense of hope.

These distorted perceptions of time can cloud our ability to make decisions. An example of this is something referred to as the sunk-cost bias. This is the tendency to make decisions based on our past investment of time and money instead of considering the present situation and the likely future results.

Organizationally, this can mean reinvesting in approaches that do not achieve desired outcomes. It can also mean repeating ineffective practices because "this is how we have always done it."

## The survival brain is hyperalert to danger, perceiving threat in all possible places.

The consequences of ignoring a threat are almost always greater than the consequences of assuming the worst. Think of it this way, you could either mistake a harmless bush for a lion or mistake the hungry lion for a bush. The first mistake causes you to be needlessly cautious, the second mistake causes you to be the lion's dinner. If you misinterpret a normal response as an indicator of distress in a client, you might be labeled as overreactive. But missing a red flag can be catastrophic. To prevent a disastrous outcome, our survival brain will err on the side of overinterpreting danger. Unfortunately, this negativity bias often casts a shadow over everyday decisions.

Negativity bias more than just skews our perception of reality to overgeneralize perceived threats. It causes us to miss the positive aspects of a situation, which, in turn, limits our access to possible solutions. Therefore, our attempts to establish safety, either physically or psychologically, are increasingly challenged. The emotional toll of this mind trap can result in feelings of helplessness, hopelessness, and despair.

All four of the above-mentioned mind traps can both impact and be influenced by organizational culture. Though mind traps are the product of our brain and can drive individual behavior, the behavior of individual members influences the culture of an organization. In turn, the culture of the organization then reinforces the mind trap.

**Reflective Exercise:** Using the four mind traps described above, identify how each might be influencing your decisions, practices, or responses in ways that contribute to your compassion fatigue. What decisions, practices, or responses have been impacted by mind traps in your organization? This exercise is

58

beneficial to do in small groups with the opportunity to share results.

## Mindsets

The above-mentioned functions of the survival brain can lead to cognitive distortions or mind traps that we all occasionally fall into. However, when someone experiences chronic exposure to trauma, they can develop a stuck mindset. When this chronic exposure occurs during the developmental years of childhood, it can profoundly change their worldview.

It is helpful to examine how these beliefs develop in relation to trauma to help us better understand the root of our own stuck mindsets in order to get unstuck.

We know that when we experience a threat that we lack the resources to cope with, our brain kicks into survival mode and activates a fight, flight, or freeze response. This experience not only strengthens these response pathways, but it shapes the way our brain will perceive or interpret future experiences and stimuli. This is what is referred to as trauma reenactment. A new emotion or stressful situation is interpreted as a threat and triggers a patterned survival response.

We have already noted that helping professionals are repeatedly exposed to secondary trauma. Our response to secondary trauma is also influenced by past primary experiences with trauma.

Childhood trauma and adversity is unfortunately not a rare occurrence. As previously discussed, The Adverse Childhood Experiences (ACEs) Study showed almost two-thirds of the over 10,000 respondents identified having experienced at least one of ten examples of childhood adversity, including violence, abuse, neglect, and parental loss or separation. It should be noted that the initial study did not include significant environmental adversities, such as racism or community violence. These factors were added to subsequent ACE research projects. The Philadelphia

Urban ACE study found a higher prevalence of child adversity, with more than 37% reporting more than four of the expanded adverse experiences.

The demographic population used in the original study were insured and composed of mostly middle- to upper-income college graduates. Follow-up studies have shown the prevalence of childhood adversity among helping professionals, particularly social workers, to be slightly higher than the general population. This probably comes to no surprise to anyone reading this book. After all, many are drawn to their profession because of a personal story that feeds a sense of purpose or calling to the work they do.

We do not need to have experienced severe childhood trauma to develop a stuck mindset. Most of us do not get through childhood, let alone life, without some sort of adversity. Our mindset is also shaped by day-to-day experiences in a culture filled with covert and overt messages that support unhelpful thinking.

Additionally, relationship experiences also shape beliefs. Relationships do not need to be traumatic to be stuck in unhealthy patterns. In this way, we are impacted by the trauma of our parents by experiencing their resulting response patterns. These early relationships shape our developing worldview. Stuck mindsets are passed from generation to generation and can keep us stuck in the past of our ancestors.

Organizations also develop mindsets. Thus, organizations impacted by trauma exposure are as likely to develop stuck mindsets as an individual.

## Anatomy of a stuck mindset

Let us begin with the definition of a traumatic experience offered by Dr. Bessel van der Kolk, a pioneer in the study of trauma and trauma treatment. Van der Kolk describes traumatization as when both our internal and external resources are inadequate to cope with an external threat. There are three parts to traumatization that challenge our basic survival needs:

- There is something beyond my control (external threat)
- My protective community failed me (external resources)
- I was not capable of self-protection (internal resources)

Over time, if the traumatic exposure continues, a pervasive belief can begin to develop that:

- The world is unsafe
- I am unworthy of belonging
- I am incapable of protecting myself

This worldview paints a reality that offers no protection, something our survival brain does not tolerate well. As a result, a protective mindset can develop that believes:

- I must be in control
- My worth needs to be externally validated, so I can belong
- Someone else needs to be responsible

This stuck mindset can result in unhelpful and even destructive responses. In organizations, it can create patterns of behavior that perpetuate a negative culture. The ability to identify the underlying mindset is a first step in recognizing the unhealthy relationship patterns that can permeate an organizational culture.

# Chapter 7

# Relationship Responses

Our relationship patterns, both professional and personal, are a few of the ways we can observe our stuck mindsets. It makes sense that our triggered responses do affect our relationships. After all, relationships are where we are most vulnerable. During times of stress and vulnerability, it is easy to revert to familiar albeit unhelpful relationship roles.

In this way, the impact of exposure to secondary trauma does not just affect individuals. Flight, fight, and freeze translates into relationship responses creating a ripple effect from one interaction to the next. Since organizational culture is developed through day in and day out behaviors, culture is driven by the interactions of its people.

## The reenactment triangle

You might be familiar with the drama triangle (also known as the reenactment triangle) introduced by Dr. Stephen Karpman decades ago. Karpman identifies three roles we take in unhealthy interactions (victim, persecutor, and rescuer.) This triangle is a useful tool for understanding the impact of trauma and adversity on relationship dynamics.

The reason the triangle is sometimes referred to as the reenactment triangle is that past experiences create patterned responses to relationship stressors. These responses can be as much driven by our past traumas as the current situation.

Like all triggered survival responses, the three roles of the drama/reenactment triangle (persecutor, rescuer, and victim) represent the fight, flight, and freeze response as they occur in behavioral interactions.

In the role of the persecutor, we have been triggered into a fight response. Common persecutor responses involve threats, name-calling, labeling, vilifying, and other coercive behavior.

In the role of rescuer, we have usually been triggered into a flight response. Rescuer behavior is a veiled attempt to flee an uncomfortable emotion or circumstance. Common rescuer behavior involves fixing other people's problems so we do not have to watch them struggle. Rescuer behavior can also involve avoiding conflict, both internal and external, by pacifying the situation.

Finally, in the role of the victim we have been triggered into a freeze response. Common victim responses involve passively waiting for someone else to solve their problem for them or failing to take responsibility for their own actions.

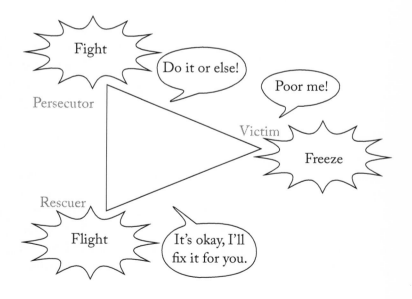

Helping professionals are constantly drawn into this triangle by others that have experienced relationship trauma. Often, depending on their role, they step into the relationship already responding as a rescuer or a persecutor. Once in the triangle, you are more likely to be triggered into any of the three behavioral responses.

> **Important note:** Remember, there is a profound difference between being victimized, past victimization, and present victim responses. If you or someone else is currently being victimized, then you might need to take a protective action or seek help. In this context, we are referring to when something in the past is causing you to think and respond in the role of a victim. As a helping professional, you cannot rescue someone from a past victimization.

Organizations, too, can react in these roles. Helping organizations often enter relationships with service recipients in a rescuer or persecutor role. Many have real or perceived authority that creates an unbalanced power dynamic. At the same time, they also must answer to restrictive regulating or governing bodies. This unbalanced power dynamic leaves them set up to be triggered into a triangle response.

Most of us can identify times in our work where we have found ourselves responding from the role of the victim, persecutor, or rescuer. Helping professionals will likely recognize these unhealthy patterns in interactions with clients, coworkers, managers, and even in their personal relationships. However, recognizing the roles of the triangle is only the beginning to building resilience on a path to healthier relationships.

We must also recognize that the reenactment triangle is a survival response impacted by underlying thoughts and emotions. It reflects a stuck way of thinking developed as a response to trauma exposure and often reinforced in today's culture. Although there are three distinct roles in the triangle, all roles are triggered by the same stuck mindset we discussed in the previous chapter.

These beliefs are rooted in our past experiences and world-views that begin to develop when we are denied our basic needs of belonging, competency, and control. If we reexamine Van der Kolk's definition of trauma as an external threat in which we lack the external or internal resources to cope, we can see the breakdown of all three of these needs. Something has happened beyond my control, my protective community failed me, and I was not able to protect myself. Over time, a pervasive belief can begin to develop, causing us to believe that the world is unsafe. I am unworthy of belonging, and I am not capable of protecting myself. This dangerous pervasive belief produces a protective belief: I must be in control, I need to be validated to belong, or someone else needs to be responsible.

This protective mindset can begin to permeate our beliefs about relationships. They often manifest into unhelpful thinking patterns that keep us locked into triangle response patterns. Such thinking includes:

- **Blaming:** Someone needs to be blamed or punished to control the situation.
- **Entitlement:** I am owed something, and I need external validation of my worth.
- **Helplessness:** I do not have the power to change things for the better and this inability is unchangeable.

When faced with interpersonal conflict, the thought patterns of the protective mindset heighten the perception of threat and increase the likelihood of a response from any one of the triangle roles. Any relationship response, be it from the role of persecutor, rescuer, or victim can be rooted in any or all three of these unhelpful thinking patterns.

# The root of blaming

Blaming is a method of controlling. If we can pinpoint a cause and effect relationship to negative events, we can control them. The alternative is that things happen arbitrarily and are beyond our control. Although blaming can be directed toward oneself, most often the finger pointing is aimed at an external entity or other. Attached to blaming is the need to make someone accountable through a punitive or sometimes manipulative response.

Blaming is often embedded in the culture of human service organizations facing seemingly unsolvable problems. This, in turn, reinforces the experiences of leaders, middle managers, frontline staff, and the people we serve.

# The root of entitlement

Some people assume that entitled thinking comes from having everything given to you. But the belief that we are owed something from those around us is far more common and complex. More often, entitled thinking is rooted in deprivation. When something or someone has deprived us of a developmental need or sense of worth, we seek external validation to get it back. Though entitlement can stem from having everything given to you, one could argue that denial of the opportunity to struggle is also a deprivation of a developmental need.

Our sense of worth is shaken when we experience an interruption or deprivation of emotional and physical needs. This can occur in the form of abuse and neglect or other traumatic experiences, including experiences of racism and systemic oppression. Sometimes we receive overt or covert messages from others that negatively shape our perception.

A work culture that consistently undermines the worth of their employees or workloads that create more opportunities for failure than success continue to undermine a sense of worth. An organization's culture can also send strong messages about the worth of others, including those in the service community.

## The root of helplessness

It is easier to identify how helplessness can develop in relation to past experiences, especially those that took place in childhood before capabilities are fully developed. However, when we are stuck in the past, we can fail to see that our internal resources have grown.

Helping professionals are often exposed to situations that can reinforce this helplessness. Not everyone can be saved. Sometimes even the best efforts result in dire results for the people they are trying to help. They bear witness to larger systemic problems that they feel powerless to change. One child-welfare worker makes this point as she talks about her experience:

> It's hard enough to hear stories of children enduring trauma at the hands of those that should have protected them, but the worst is seeing firsthand the trauma inflicted by a broken system and knowing that I am a part of that system.

Organizations chronically exposed to trauma tend to develop relationship patterns within the reenactment triangle. Managers use coercion in an attempt to gain compliance. Workers develop a learned helplessness in response to agency needs, and leadership stifles communication in an attempt to silence dissent. These internal patterns both influence and perpetuate unhelpful interactions with their service community and the greater system.

**Reflective Exercise:** Using the triangle, identify three relationship interactions in which you responded out of one of the roles. Try to identify the emotions and mindsets that might have triggered this response.

It always seems easier to identify unhealthy relationship responses in others. To be an agent of change, we need to be able to recognize them in ourselves and in our organizations. The work of the helping professional is to get to the root of his or her own responses.

## Shifting relationship mindsets

The more we are triggered, the more vulnerable we are to mind traps that can keep us stuck in the triangle roles. Polarized thinking can lead to a perspective that these roles are the only options. I must be a persecutor, if I do not want to be a victim; if I am not rescuing, I must be the bad guy, and so on.

Here I would like to explore the mindset that can begin to free us from unhealthy relationship patterns.

Since stuck mindsets are rooted in threats to our basic human needs, unstuck mindsets involve beliefs that restore a sense of autonomy, belonging, and competence.

- **Ownership:** I am responsible for my own feelings, thoughts, and behaviors (and no one else's).
- **Humility:** I am human, and all humans have flaws, and all humans have worth.
- **Change:** I am not bound by my past abilities; everyone is capable of growth and change.

When we can identify stuck thinking and unhealthy relationship patterns, we create an opportunity for a different response. However, mindsets can be deeply embedded. Change needs to come from more than simply shifting our thinking. It requires different relationship experiences, responses, and habits.

When we respond as a victim, persecutor, or rescuer, we are also crossing a boundary by attempting to control what is not ours to control in the form of responsibility and emotions. We will explore boundaries as a skill and as a necessary practice for cultivating compassion in a later chapter.

# Chapter 8
# Self-Regulation

Our awareness of our cognitive, emotional, and body responses to trauma exposure helps us to recognize when we are experiencing compassion fatigue; or to return to our initial analogy, to recognize when our circuit breaker has been tripped. Our first response to this recognition needs to be to reset the breaker. In other words, we need to engage in self-regulation to restore a sense of safety.

But first, we need to remember the bottom-up order in which the brain is going to respond to threatening or perceived threatening stimuli. As stimuli come in through the brainstem, we first experience an autonomic response (increased heart rate and shortened breathing). Then as it reaches the limbic system and is interpreted as a threat the amygdala takes over sending the flight, fight, or freeze responses following the already well-formed neuronal pathways. Finally, the neocortex is engaged. This region of the brain, responsible for higher thought and reasoning, may not be involved until after the amygdala has responded. Therefore, changing the response cannot involve the neocortex alone. We also need to learn how to regulate our autonomic responses.

Remember that our autonomic nervous system is comprised of the sympathetic and parasympathetic response systems. Well-regulated people can ebb and flow between these two systems without being triggered into either flight or fight on one end of the continuum or freeze on the other. Therefore, self-regulation involves widening our tolerance of emotional triggers and increasing our awareness of our autonomic responses. We do this by employing self-regulation methods, also referred to as regulation resources.

Our neuronal system is bidirectional. Therefore, just as messages of threat trigger a physiological response. Physiological actions can trigger messages of safety back to the brain. In fact, the vagal nerve has four times as many pathways connecting the body to the brain than the other direction.

This explains why some people find chewing gum helpful when they feel anxious. Gum chewing produces saliva. Saliva is produced as part of the digestive process in the parasympathetic response. This return to normal functioning signals to the brain and communicates everything is all right.

Facial and vocal muscles are also part of the parasympathetic nervous system. Therefore, humming or singing can stimulate a return to parasympathetic state. These types of regulation resources are what we call bottom up, in reference to where they originate in our neurological system.

Examples of top-down regulation resources would include self-talk, visualizing a place of safety or connection, naming feelings, or reaching out to an external resource to process or challenge distorted thinking.

Regulation resources can further be characterized not only as top-down or bottom-up but as calming or connecting. Calming to bring us back from a fight or flight response, connecting to engage us from a freeze response of disconnect. Both types of resources bring us back to a state of safety.

Breathing exercises are great examples of a bottom-up regulating resource that can assist in both calming and connecting. When we take a long deep breath that fills our lungs with oxygen, we are engaging a connective response. A long slow exhale, however, engages our parasympathetic response and has a calming effect. Thus, learning to pay attention to our breathing and practicing deliberate deep breathing exercises is an effective regulating resource at our disposal.

Similarly, mindfulness is a set of practices that improve the ability to focus on the present, increasing our awareness and accepting of the now. Mindfulness techniques offer a variety of exercises that provide regulation resources in all four quadrants of top-down or bottom-up and calming or connecting.

> **Reflective Exercise:** No doubt, human service organizations and helping professionals already have at least some regulation resources at their disposal. Using the attachment at the end of this chapter, begin by identifying the regulation methods in each quadrant that you have successfully used in the past. Conducting this activity in a group broadens the available resources as people share their current skill sets. It is also important to identify skill gaps in any of the quadrants. Organizations can support this effort by providing opportunities to learn and practice new self-regulation skills.

Ultimately, the goal is to be able to identify when we have been triggered and use these regulation resources to restore our sense of safety. In other words, reset the breaker.

Though the need is not just for individuals. Organizations, too, must reset and restore, thus, the need for organizational awareness.

# Regulation Resources

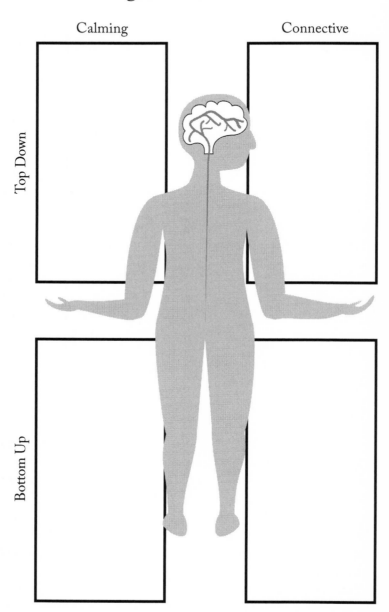

# Chapter 9
# Organizational Awareness

As we increase our awareness of compassion fatigue in helping professionals, it is important to examine the impact of chronic exposure to secondary trauma on organizations that serve those who have been traumatized.

It is not just our own trauma history and the exposure to secondary trauma that keep us stuck in unhealthy mindsets and response patterns. Our mindset is also shaped by day-to-day experiences in a culture filled with covert and overt messages that support a stuck mindset. Organizations that serve traumatized people develop their own trauma histories, mindsets, and response patterns.

## Organizational development

Since organizations are made up of human beings, they develop in much the same way. Our understanding of the brain and brain development can provide insight into understanding organizational development. The brain is a working model for all living organisms and relationships, including organizations and communities. Therefore, let us refer to the design elements of the brain as described in chapter two and examine how they relate to organizations.

The brain has two developmental drivers, the blueprint mapped by our DNA and our experiences throughout life.

Likewise, organizations usually begin with a purpose and a plan, but they are profoundly influenced by their experiences.

The brain is designed with goals to both thrive and survive. Likewise, most social service agencies or helping institutions have a stated goal or mission to serve the community in a manner that has positive impact. Therefore, their programs, strategies, and actions are designed to fulfill their mission statement. However, to accomplish their mission, they must also achieve sustainability. That is, they must survive to serve another day. This unwritten goal of survival can become as much or more of a driver than the mission. This is especially true for organizations that live in a climate of constant external threat. Funding cuts, restrictive regulations, and external pressures to conform to flawed processes are all everyday challenges to organizations. Even other agencies that share the same mission can be viewed as predators in a world where there is competition for funding.

Additionally, by design, these organizations are repeatedly exposed to the secondary trauma of those they serve. As this exposure takes its toll on the individuals that make up the organizations, burned-out staff and constant turnover become ongoing challenges that add to the toxic stress of the environment.

In addition to a climate of external threats and chronic exposure to secondary trauma and stress, helping institutions are vulnerable to and often experience primary traumatic events. This can include loss of programs, layoffs, and even death or severe injury to an employee or client.

Like the human brain, organizations interpret data to help them achieve their goals. Much like individuals, organizations develop mindsets that are shaped by an experience with an unsafe world. Often these unspoken beliefs can contradict the professed organizational values. These mindsets, in turn, can drive the agencies' response patterns. This can cause the agency to be profoundly more reactive than proactive.

The beliefs and practices of the people in the organization is what forms its culture. That is, the values and beliefs that are consistently demonstrated throughout the organization. (These may differ from the values hanging on the wall.)

Relationships are as vital to the health and healing of an organization as they are to an individual. Organizational trauma histories also impact organizational relationships, both internally and externally. Relationship patterns can be a source of retraumatization or they can be a source of healing. Therefore, an understanding of relationship roles and responses is a necessary part of an organizational assessment.

In the same way the brain's design impacts the individual, the above elements factor into the development of present-day organizational culture. Most helping organizations have a past that includes exposure to primary trauma as well as secondary trauma. We must acknowledge that many also have histories of inflicting trauma and perpetuating institutional racism. These experiences, too, become embedded in the current culture. Failure to acknowledge any or all of these wounds leaves workers to carry the burden of trauma they cannot even name.

## Symptoms of a compassion fatigued organization

Just as with individuals, recognition of the symptoms of organizational compassion fatigue is a core step in creating a compassionate culture. Below is a list of symptoms that are far from exclusive but can begin the process of organizational awareness.

Cognitive symptoms:
- **Scarcity thinking:** Is the organization generous with its resources and does it prioritize, making sure programs and staff have the resources they need to be successful? *Or is there a constant pressure to find ways to cut expenses and make do with less?*

- **Finger pointing:** Do leaders and staff step up to take responsibility for their part when things go wrong? *Or is there a scramble to assign blame elsewhere?*
- **Failure to learn from mistakes:** Does the organization embrace both successes and failures as learning opportunities? *Or do they keep repeating the same mistakes?*
- **Fixed potential:** Does the organization develop and inspire employees at all levels? *Or does leadership see some as having fixed roles and capabilities?*
- **Denial:** Do leaders have an accurate perception of the challenges their organization might face? *Or are they unaware of the struggles of their employees and the needs of the community?*
- **Polarization:** Do all members have a sense of ownership? *Or is there a strong us-against-them mentality between management and front line, different departments, and even staff and clients?*

Emotional symptoms:

- **Conflict:** Are conflicts viewed as learning opportunities and addressed in a timely manner? *Or do they go unresolved, allowing anger to fester?*
- **Fear:** Do employees feel safe in the knowledge that they will be treated fairly? *Or is fear the primary motivator?*
- **Emotional stifling:** Are there healthy avenues for emotional expression? *Or do negative emotions surface in the form of low morale, absenteeism, and high turnover?*
- **Numbing:** Is leadership attuned to the emotional pulse of employees? *Or is there a failure to validate this human response?*
- **Reactionary responses:** Does the organization make value-based decisions guided by future expectations? *Or do they react to situations based on past negative perceptions and emotions?*

Behavioral Symptoms:

- **Punitive practices:** Does the organization encourage accountability through clear expectations, learning opportunities and choice? *Or does it try to control behavior through punitive methods?*
- **Lack of transparency:** Is information flow bidirectional, clear, and open? *Or is needed information kept hidden?*
- **Lack of innovation:** Does the organization support questioning and experimentation? *Or are employees expected to blindly follow rigid procedures?*
- **Limited lines of communication:** Is the leadership open to learning from all members of the organization? *Or do they only value and rely on the opinions of an elite few?*
- **Disconnect:** Do practices accurately reflect agency values? *Or do the actions of leaders and practitioners routinely contradict professed values?*
- **Lack of purpose:** Is there a clear connection between the work being done and the mission of the organization? *Or do people wonder about the purpose of what they are told to do?*

Conducting an organizational assessment includes gathering many perspectives regarding the above symptoms. It is important to recognize that the perspective of the frontline workforce might be different from that of leadership. It is also helpful to know how clients and community partners perceive the organization. But just as we ask the trauma-informed question, "What happened to them?" when referring to individuals we serve, we must ask the same question when assessing the organization.

The irony of all this is that organizations designed to facilitate a compassionate response to social problems begin to feel like places that hold no space for compassion to thrive. But this is not an accurate reflection of an organization's heart. It is merely a symptom of the same compassion fatigue experienced by the people it employs. The solution, therefore, lies in cultivating a culture of compassion.

Part III

# Keeping the Lights on:

Cultivating Compassion

Once I familiarized myself with my breaker box, I became quite good at flipping the switch to restore power, and I had a lot of practice. That first year I lived in my new house, I probably tripped the breaker once or twice a week. At first, it felt empowering to have a problem I knew how to solve. But eventually, it grew tiresome.

A friend who knew a bit more than I did about electrical wiring suggested there may be a bigger problem. Sure enough, I discovered that as my older home had been updated over the years, new outlets had been added to the lines in a way that was causing an overload. I had to have an electrician do some rewiring to fix it. It still trips on occasion, but not nearly as often as it used to.

In the same sense, self-awareness and regulation can help us to "flip the breaker" to restore compassion. However, this does not keep us from tripping the breaker again and again. Building resilience to secondary trauma requires exercising our "compassion muscle." Individually, this means developing new response patterns to "rewire the brain." Organizationally, this requires changing day-to-day practices to shift agency culture. Both involve reinforcing skill sets and mindsets practiced over time that cultivate compassion.

The following chapters examine six skill sets for cultivating compassion:

- Establishing boundaries
- Exercising empathy
- Expressing gratitude
- Processing
- Connecting
- Planning for self-care

We will explore each of these skills from the perspective of the individual helping professional, offering insight as to why they are important and how they can be cultivated. We will also examine how these same skills can be supported by organizations and embedded in organizational culture.

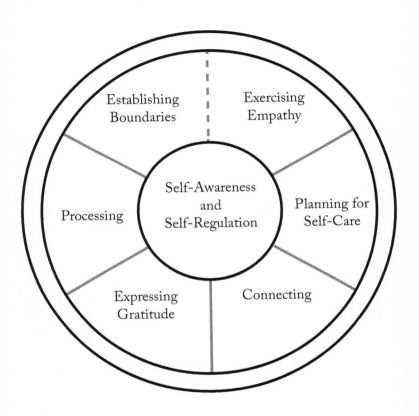

# Chapter 10
# Establishing Boundaries

Relationships are a fundamental part of being human. We are wired to connect with each other as a source of both healing and survival. With every relationship, personal or professional, comes the need for boundaries. Boundaries are the invisible lines that keep us physically and emotionally safe while effectively functioning. They govern what we are willing to do and not do, say and hear, and give and receive. But what do they have to do with cultivating compassion?

I often joke in my trainings that I have good relationship skills, as long as no one else is in the room. I will be honest; there are times when I feel provoked to respond in ways that are not so compassionate. Afterward, I can usually identify the underlying emotion or perceived threat that triggered my response. But I am also surprised at how often it was precipitated by having my boundaries crossed. It is probably more accurate to say, my response was precipitated by a boundary I failed to clearly set.

Boundaries keep us safe. As humans, safety, or at least the perception of safety, allows us to choose compassion as our response.

Helping professionals, by nature of their role, are constantly asked to ignore their own boundaries and the boundaries of others. They are faced with helping others who never asked for their help, roles that are not clearly defined, and tasks that require giving more of themselves than what feels healthy or safe.

For helping professionals who wish to be compassionate, the skill of understanding and establishing healthy boundaries is essential. The ability to establish healthy boundaries not only helps to restore safety, it is the foundation of every other skill set addressed in this section to combat compassion fatigue.

## Understanding boundaries

Boundaries come in many forms. We tend to initially think of them in terms of personal space. But boundaries are also needed for resources, time and energy, information and opinions, roles and responsibilities, and emotions. They can vary from relationship to relationship, depending on the need. For example, I might share my feelings about a personal relationship with my sister, but not my dry cleaner.

As with most skill sets, boundaries begin with knowing yourself. This not only involves identifying our emotional triggers but also exploring relationship values and mindsets.

Remember that our mindsets hold beliefs and messages about how the world operates in the context of relationships. Sometimes these internal messages can be powerful barriers to setting healthy boundaries. *What are the mindsets as identified in Part II that interfere with your ability to establish healthy boundaries?*

Setting boundaries can be difficult for someone who has had their boundaries violated in the past. Often, they come with feelings of resentment, helplessness, and shame. Unfortunately, not setting them allows these difficult feelings to go unresolved. It also creates situations that reinforce an unhealthy view of relationships and robs us of the healing properties healthy relationships can provide.

## Trauma and boundaries

In chapter seven we explored how traumatic relationship experiences can lead to a stuck mindset that can trigger a response in the roles of victim, rescuer, and persecutor. None of these roles are effective. (Remember, we cannot rescue someone from their past trauma.) More importantly, each of these roles represent a boundary violation in some way.

When we respond as a victim, persecutor, or rescuer, we are crossing a boundary by attempting to control what is not ours to control in the form of responsibility and emotions. For example, both the persecutor and the rescuer violate someone else's right to power and control of his or her own life. The rescuer can also cross a boundary by taking on another's responsibility. Sometimes, people in the victim role can shift some of the responsibility away from themselves and onto others. We also cross emotional boundaries when we attempt to manipulate or control someone else's emotional response because it makes us uncomfortable.

Whether responding from the role of persecutor (fight), rescuer (flight), or victim (freeze), we often choose protective devices that perpetuate conflict, trauma, and a stuck world view. These protective devices include coercion, manipulation, and denial.

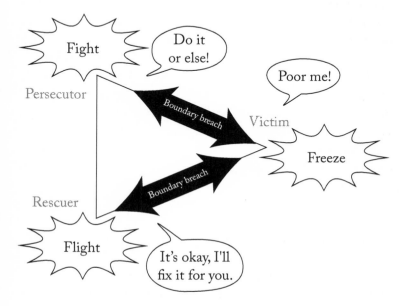

The use of coercion, manipulation, and denial crosses boundaries and damages relationships. When we respond with coercion, we are attempting to exert power over another, thus violating a boundary. This includes threats and punitive reactions.

A punitive response is the deliberate infliction of a pain, be it physical or emotional, in response to a past behavior, although, sometimes negative consequences are the natural result of poor decisions. If the decision is informed and made freely, the negative consequence is not the same as a punishment. Often, punishment is justified as an attempt to control future behavior. This reactionary response fails to recognize the responsibility of the individual to choose his or her own behavior and take responsibility for the natural consequences of that choice.

Manipulation, like coercion, is an attempt to control the thoughts, feelings, and behaviors of another. Because of its more passive nature, manipulation can often be more difficult to identify than coercion. It still represents a boundary violation and can be, nonetheless, just as destructive.

Manipulation is often justified as "for the good of another." This reactionary response fails to recognize the right and responsibility of individuals to experience their own emotions and choose their own response. Even seemingly helpful attempts to reframe a painful experience can be a manipulative attempt to control another's emotional response.

Another device used to control another is denial. Denial can be a form of manipulation or coercion. This can take the form of denial of information or resources or it can be the denial of responsibility or emotion.

An example might be a leader denying information to employees to prevent an uncomfortable emotional response. The leader might even justify this action as benevolent because he or she is sparing employees the fear or worry that might come from knowing about an impending threat. This is a common example of rescuer behavior. It is a violation of a boundary to decide for another person what they can and cannot handle. In doing so, we are not only denying someone the right to their own emotional response, but we can also be denying them the opportunity to prepare for a potential reality. More important is the recognition that denial of information is often more of a protective response for the rescuer than those they are attempting to rescue.

In contrast, responses that offer choice and transparency avoid boundary breaches. These responses promote the restoration of autonomy, belonging, and competency. Thus, the response roles in the trauma triangle shift from persecutor to coach, rescuer to ally, and victim to thriver.

Choice and transparency are the difference between an ally response and a manipulative response. For example, instead of an unsolicited reframe "You should be thankful that at least you still have a job," an ally response might be, "I can understand your disappointment, when you are ready, I would be happy to

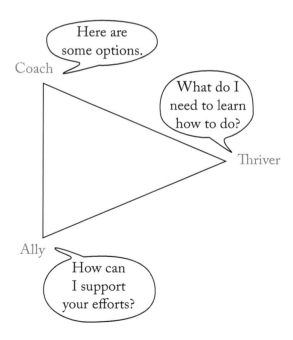

help you identify some of the good things you still have to look forward to."

Choice and transparency are also the difference between punishment and accountability. Instead of, "If you don't get with the program, there will be disciplinary action," a coaching response might be, "These are the requirements of this job, if you choose to continue working in this program, let's discuss what that will need to look like and how I can help you be successful." Notice that the second response is not any less accountable than the first. It just recognizes the boundaries of responsibilities and clarifies the expectations of the manager.

## Establishing boundaries

There are several steps involved in the process of developing healthy and effective boundaries including:

- Identifying needs
- Setting limits
- Recognizing cues
- Clarifying

Establishing boundaries is an ongoing process and each of these steps is practiced and repeated as necessary throughout our lifetime.

## Identifying needs

Although setting healthy boundaries is an essential step for any relationship, they do not have to be set in stone. They can change as relationship needs change. It is important to ask yourself if your current boundaries are working to keep you safe and allowing you to be effective. In healthy relationships, these conversations might need to involve both people.

We begin by determining what is needed in each relationship to be safe and effective. Keep in mind that needs are different for varying relationships. Sometimes it is necessary to start by identifying categories of relationships:

- **Close relationships:** These are people you know well and for a long time and are involved in or concerned with most areas of your life. You provide support to each other when needed and there is a commitment to be there for each other in both good and bad times. This can include family members, intimate partners, or long-time friends.

- **Friend relationships:** People who you know well enough to list their qualities and who know you enough to do the same. This is a two-way, supportive relationship, but support is optional and not necessarily expected or required. These relationships might provide in only one area of your life (family, social, work, church), or sometimes they may cross over into more than one area.

- **Resource relationships:** People with whom we have a necessary relationship because we provide each other with a resource. The relationship might be either one-way or two-way support. Examples might be your boss, someone who works for you, some coworkers, your doctor, a client, etc.

- **Acquaintances:** People we know but either do not know well enough to be in any of the other categories or we choose not to put them in any other category.

Recognizing the type of relationship can keep us from blurring the boundaries. It also helps us to better identify the needs of that relationship.

**Practice Exercise:** Use the following questions to help identify relationship needs for each identified relationship or relationship category. Remember that boundaries are bidirectional and so are needs. Therefore, it is important to consider what the other person's needs are as well as your own.

What do you each need to accomplish through this relationship?

What do you need to know or learn from each other?

What kind of support do you need from each other?

What is the most important goal of this relationship for each of you?

If identifying needs is a struggle, go back to self-awareness. Sometimes it is helpful to begin by keeping a journal of times when we feel unclear boundaries might be the root of a problem. Ask yourself what was needed to make the interaction more successful.

# Setting limits

Limits include what you are willing and not willing to do, give and not give, and reveal and not reveal. In other words, what we will say yes to and what we will say no to.

Our polarized thinking and negative bias can lead us to describe boundary limits as either good or bad. More specifically, we tend to associate loose boundaries as bad and tight boundaries as good. This is not always the case. When we label boundaries as good or bad, it puts a value judgment on someone else's boundaries that might be more a reflection of our own comfort level.

All people have boundaries that slide along intersecting continuums of loose or tight and clear or unclear. What makes a boundary healthy is not whether its limits are loose or tight, but whether it is clearly communicated, adaptable to varying situations or relationships, and allows us to function safely. Unhealthy boundaries can have limits that are either too loose or too tight, and most often, they are not communicated in understandable ways. Responses to potential boundary breaches can range from extreme and inflexible to nonexistent. They can create an unsafe situation, or, if they serve to maintain safety, they often do so at the expense of the relationship.

Setting limits involves identifying what you will say yes to and what you will say no to in each boundary area. These limits will vary for each type of relationship and depend on those relationship needs previously identified.

Remember, limits do not have to be set in stone. They can change as relationship needs change.

**Practice Exercise:** Use the worksheet provided at the end of this chapter to set limits in what you are willing to say yes or no to. Think about what you would do or have done, give our get, and reveal or hear.

## Recognizing cues

How do you know when someone has crossed a boundary or when you have crossed someone else's? This involves being attuned to our emotions and body responses to having our boundaries crossed. But it also requires the insight to interpret another's frustrating behavior as a messy attempt to set a boundary.

Most of us have experienced our boundaries being crossed in one way or the other. Remember that boundaries are not just physical. We need boundaries for what we reveal (information, emotions, opinions), what we give (resources, time, energy), and what we do (responsibilities, values, and personal space).

We need to recognize that boundaries are a two-way street. Even someone with clear boundaries can accidently cross someone else's. But, since people with unhealthy boundaries tend to respond in messy ways, sometimes we do not even recognize their response as a boundary at all. Instead, it is interpreted as hostility, indifference, or rejection. Having healthy boundaries means respecting the boundaries of others, even if they struggle to communicate them.

Learning to recognize the emotional and physical cues for when our boundaries are crossed is a skill set that may need to be developed or fine-tuned.

Sometimes the breach is so subtle it is not consciously noticed. The helping professional can only describe an uncomfortable feeling or sensation around certain people, without naming the source of this discomfort. When this occurs, it is helpful to review the different types of boundaries to see if they can identify one or more ways in which their personal boundary has been crossed. When someone has boundaries that are considerably looser than our own, it is easy for ours to be breached, particularly if they are unaware of a boundary that has not been clearly defined and communicated.

The reverse is true when someone's boundary is tighter than our own. The risk then becomes that we might cross a boundary we did not recognize was there. In this case, the cues given by the other person may not be direct and easily deciphered. Behavioral responses might be subtle or mismatched. In which case, they can be misinterpreted as indifference or even hostility. When we pick up on a cue from another that seems like an inappropriate response, instead of analyzing motive and intent, ask the question, "Did I cross this person's boundary in some way?" Practicing this level of self-inquiry helps us to hone our attunement skills.

## Clarifying

We clarify our boundaries both directly and indirectly through our words and actions. Sometimes, when our boundaries are crossed or about to be crossed, it is necessary to make a clear boundary statement. A clear boundary statement involves identifying the breach, communicating your need, and offering a suggestion of what would be acceptable. Here are some examples.

Information Boundary:
- That is too personal. I would feel more comfortable talking about something less personal to get to know each other. What are some of your interests or hobbies?

Time Boundary:
- That would mean working through dinner. I have set aside dinnertime to be with my family. I am willing to come in early tomorrow to catch up instead.
- This is becoming more than I can offer. I need to reserve my time on weekends for my family. I could help out an hour a month during the week.

Responsibility Boundary:
- That is not my responsibility. I want to see you accomplish that on your own. I would be happy to walk you through how it is done.

Emotional Boundary:
- You have shared a lot of strong feelings today. I am confident you will be able to work through this.
- We seem to only talk about negative things. I need to

be able to share positive emotions, too. Let's make sure we set aside time to talk about possible solutions.

Boundary statements should be kept short. You are not required to overly explain why you have a boundary.

**Practice Exercise:** It is helpful to have boundary statements ready and practiced ahead of time. Using the same worksheet used for setting limits, write at least one boundary statement in each category. Choose the boundaries that are most often challenged in your work.

Just communicating boundaries to others is not always enough. We need to be responsible for keeping the boundaries we set.

Emotional boundaries can be especially challenging for helping professionals. To be truly empathetic, we need to be fully present for those we serve. But it is crucial that we remember that their problems are their problems and not ours to take home. (Most of us have our own problems to deal with.)

I remember once, early in my career, becoming so distressed about a family I was working with who was going to be evicted. One night, I had a dream that they were all sleeping on the floor of my apartment. When I woke up, I knew that I was not setting a healthy emotional boundary.

Overtime, I learned ways to keep these boundaries from becoming blurred. I found that it was helpful to establish some sort of separation ritual that allowed me to define the emotional boundary more clearly. I always ended my visit with something like the above boundary statement. "You have shared a lot of strong feelings today. I am confident you will be able to work through this." But when the visit was particularly emotionally laden, I did something more tangible. After I drove away from the home, I would pull over, roll down the window, and symbolically push the emotions out of my car with a wave of my hands. It was a physical reminder that these burdens were not mine to carry.

## Boundaries in organizations

Just as they are needed in any relationship, organizations also require boundaries to function safely and efficiently. Healthy organizational boundaries are clearly communicated, adaptable to needs, and allow helping professionals to thrive. Unfortunately, unhealthy relationship patterns can lead to unhealthy boundaries. Boundaries can be crossed in both their external and internal relationships.

Here are just some examples of how organizational boundaries are crossed externally:

- Allowing funders to dictate decisions for which the organization should be responsible
- Expanding into program areas outside the organization's mission or values
- Entering contract agreements that have demands beyond the organization's capacity to deliver
- Responding to community needs without consulting intended service recipients
- Reacting to public opinions or pressures without regard to organizational needs

Here are some examples of how boundaries are crossed internally in the organizational environment:

- Unclear expectations
- Unrealistic workload
- Intrusion into personal time and space
- Behavior that interferes with the work (tardiness, absenteeism, interruptions, negativity, etc.)
- Ignoring established lines of communication

For human service organizations this list also includes blurred boundaries in relation to service recipients.

In many ways, what helping professionals are asked to do in the line of duty pushes boundaries to the limits. Helping professionals are called to enter the most vulnerable and private parts of people's lives. Often, the job necessitates asking probing questions that defy the norms of most social boundaries.

Though help seekers might enter this interaction willingly, this is not always the case. For example, social workers and therapists working in the criminal justice or child welfare systems often have mandated clients. These unbalanced power dynamics make establishing healthy boundaries even more difficult.

It is important for organizations to examine the ways they hinder the ability of their employees to establish clear boundaries. A focus group of mental health practitioners shared the following examples:

> People think we automatically have good boundaries because we are professionals, but our limits are always being tested. We might spend an hour empathetically listening as someone tells us about his or her problem and then, at the end of the session, we have to collect the copay.
>
> One of the hardest things, as far as boundaries, is when you are walking a client out and you are trying to be completely present for them and the next client is already sitting in the waiting room. I do not even want to make eye contact until the first client is out the door because I need to stay present for them. But then I feel I am ignoring the one that is waiting to see me.

In both these examples, it is the structure of how they are asked to do the work that is challenging their ability to maintain clear boundaries.

The processes for which an organization establishes boundaries is the same as for individuals. It begins by identifying the relationship needs of the organization. In doing so, organizational leaders need to take care not to exclude important relationship groups in the process.

Organizations also need to clearly communicate the limits of what is and is not acceptable, based on the identified needs.

> **Practice Exercise:** Although individuals need to establish their own personal needs and limits, I recommend that program groups work together to establish boundaries using some of the same exercises used for individuals. Doing so models and supports the importance of clear boundaries. It also sets a context for frontline workers to communicate clear boundaries to service recipients.

By the way, none of this is easy work. It is, however, essential work. Learning to develop healthy boundaries is a lifelong process that almost always involves stepping outside our comfort zone. However, like every other skill set, it gets easier with practice. The results for the individual are deeper and more meaningful relationships and greater peace of mind. For an organization, boundaries create the framework for compassionate work.

| What are you willing to... | Yes | No |
|---|---|---|
| **Do** <br> or have done <br><br> Values <br> Responsibility <br> Personal Space | | |
| **Give** <br> or get <br><br> Time <br> Energy <br> Resources | | |
| **Reveal** <br> or hear <br><br> Opinion <br> Information <br> Emotions | | |

## Chapter 11

# Exercising Empathy

Just as relationships are a vital part of human survival, empathy plays a crucial role in our ability to connect with each other. At the most fundamental level, empathy allows others to respond to our distress signals, thus, perpetuating human existence. The ability to be empathetic also facilitates positive social interaction. From infancy on, social interaction is the building block for growth and learning.

Therefore, practicing empathy is an essential part of cultivating compassion. Empathy is the ability to experience another's thoughts and feelings as separate from our own.

Some neuroscientists believe empathy might be facilitated by mirror neurons. Mirror neurons are nerve cells that respond the same way when we are observing the experience of another as when we experience it ourselves Though mirror neurons are difficult to study in humans and more research is needed, they point to the idea that we are wired to develop empathy.

## Components of empathy

For the individual, empathy is a complex skill set that involves functions of the prefrontal cortex, autonomic responses and, of course, our limbic system, which is responsible for much of our emotional processing. The ability to be empathetic evolves according to our developmental experiences and can be strengthened with practice. Exercising empathy involves four components. Each of these components are skills that are developed with practice.

# Being present

The art of being present can be challenging. Being present involves listening with focus. Of course, this is not always as easy as it sounds. We might think we are good listeners but most of the time would-be listeners are distracted by their own agenda. Sometimes what we hear triggers us to either change the subject or tell the person how to fix the problem. Whenever we start giving advice or talking about something else, we are no longer listening.

> **Practice Exercise:** To rid yourself of distractions, try grounding yourself in the present. Sometimes it helps to take a deep breath and focus on the here and now. Take notice of the chair you are in, the temperature of the room, and most importantly the person you are with.
>
> Focus on the content of what the other person is saying. I find it helpful to visualize the story as it is being told. When there is a pause, instead of shifting the conversation, elicit more information. Ask, "What happened next?" or "Tell me more about...."

Another challenge to being present is the discomfort many of us have with silence, especially silence that is laden with emotion. Sometimes people need a moment to process their thoughts or reflect on what was just said. When there is silence, resist the urge to fill it with unnecessary words. Practicing self-regulation, as addressed in chapter eight, increases our ability to sit with uncomfortable emotions without the need to immediately respond.

## Suspending judgment

Judgment is an important function of our brain. As we mentioned earlier, our brain is skillful at scanning for data to interpret and analyze in order to make decisions and choose responses. Judgment is the process of drawing conclusions from the information that is available. This includes our own perceptions. Empathy requires an emotional connection that goes beyond analysis and involves emotional processing as well as autonomic responses. It is important to distinguish between a judgment and identifying the emotion that the other is experiencing.

Judgment and empathy are often seen as opposing functions. Although it might not be necessary or possible to completely disengage our judgment function. It is helpful to suspend judgment to allow for a more empathetic response.

Suspending judgment can be more challenging in some situations than others. Often, human behavior can be difficult to understand and might trigger strong negative emotions. In this case, initial attempts to practice empathy can sometimes trigger a judgmental response. As we struggle to identify with the motive, the brain shifts easily into judgment mode.

**Practice Exercise:** In situations where you struggle to stay out of judgment, try momentarily letting go of the need for an explanation. Instead, it is more helpful to remind ourselves of the universal things that make us human. The following list provides some examples.

- All people make mistakes
- All people are trying to survive
- All people want to feel good about themselves
- All people want to belong
- All people feel pain

In these ways, this person is no different than you or anyone else.

This exercise can be practiced using movie clips with challenging characters and circumstances. In my training experience, I have found that, at first, participants struggle staying out of judgment, even when they are instructed to identify the character's emotions. After reading out loud the above list and processing in relation to the movie character, they can more easily shift away from judgment.

## Perspective taking

Often, we think of empathy as the ability to stand in another's shoes. Too often, we do this by thinking about how we would respond if in the other person's situation. True empathetic perception taking goes much deeper than this. It involves not only standing in another's shoes but standing in their history of experiences and their current emotional responses. It is not about how we would feel but how they feel.

Fundamentally, human beings are egocentric. Even deliberate attempts to take on another's perspective are filtered through our own lens of understanding. Therefore, perspective taking is a skill that requires practice to develop.

To take on another perspective requires the executive function of flexible thinking as well as the ability to distinguish one's own perspective from another.

## Emotional attunement

Perspective taking alone does not define empathy. True empathy requires a connection at an emotional level. The ability to identify and process the emotion of another is called emotional attunement.

Though attunement is primarily a function of the limbic system, studies have revealed a connection between empathy and facial muscles. It is a natural response to mimic the behaviors, mannerisms and even voice tone of those with whom we interact.

In studies where subjects mimicked facial expressions, emotional responses increased. Additionally, people who experienced having their facial expressions mirrored, displayed more cooperative behavioral responses. Further research has shown that impairment of this ability can limit the ability to recognize emotions.

The relationship between empathy and facial expression became evident to me quite by accident during a training exercise I did on mirroring. I handed out emotion word cards and instructed participants in pairs to take turns expressing an emotion without using words. Their partner was instructed to mirror the expression and then guess the emotion. They usually struggled with the task. At first, I thought this was because there are so many subtle nuances to nonverbal emotional expressions (such as worried versus afraid.) Then, I noticed that they were not mirroring the expression before jumping to the guessing part. (Perhaps, they were too eager for the activity to pay attention to instructions.) To better monitor the activity to ensure the instructions were followed, I changed the structure of the exercise. I turned it into a large group circle activity in which participants expressed their emotions to the next person and so on down the line. In this way, I could remind the participant each time to first mirror the expression physically. I then asked them to try to name the emotion. To my surprise, the group named the correct emotion first try every time. I have since continued to do this exercise the same way with similar results. I have even divided the participants into two groups in larger classes. I instruct one group to first mirror and then identify the feeling, and the second to just try to identify the feeling based on the expression. Inevitably, the group that mirrors can identify the emotion on the first try at a higher rate.

Though, this "experiment" is hardly scientific, I think it illustrates something important about attunement. Naming a feeling is a function of the prefrontal cortex. True emotional attunement requires engaging the limbic system. Also, it is a reminder that our neuronal system is bidirectional. A body response can provoke an emotion just as an emotion can provoke a body response.

So when practicing empathy, it might help to remember to "put your face into it." That is, relax your face muscles and allow them to naturally mirror the expression of the person with whom you are connecting.

> **Practice Exercise:** Another way to strengthen emotional attunement is with reflective response. Most of what people say has an emotional undertone. Next time you are in a conversation, try listening to how the person feels about what he or she is telling you. Then, echo it back. "You must have been really proud." or "That must have been painful."

The successful practice of empathy leads to a clearer understanding of what the other person needs and values. A good way to check for effectiveness when practicing empathy is to summarize what the person needs and what is important to them based on what you heard. Ask if you heard correctly and allow clarification if necessary.

## Organizational Practice

An organization exercises empathy by encouraging individuals to practice empathy. This can be accomplished through formal training and skill-building activities. It can also be accomplished through modeling. Individual leaders that model empathy encourage the practice at all levels. An empathetic leader creates empathetic supervisors. Modeling empathy in supervision, supports exercising empathy with clients.

However, the individual practice of empathy is only part of the equation. To develop organizational empathy, an organization needs to examine policy and practice for evidence of and barriers to exercising empathy. Using the components of empathy, let us look at what that looks like from an organizational perspective.

## Being present

An organization that is constantly in crisis mode and putting out fires will struggle much the way an individual who is not emotionally regulated will struggle being present in a conversation.

So for an organization, being present simply means regularly examining priorities to ensure that the needs of their workforce and service recipients do not get moved too far down the list of things they are paying attention to.

## Suspending judgment

As stated before, judgment is a function of the human brain. So, too, is regular data analysis to a human service organization. Outcome measurements and data indicators can be used to effectively assess organizational impact and is usually a requirement of funders and regulatory entities.

However, sometimes organizations misuse or misunderstand the purpose of data collection. The result is that people are being judged, or feel they are being judged, for outcomes and indicators that are not completely or at all under their control. This can have a trickle-down effect from upper management to the client that leaves little room for the practice of empathy.

## Perspective taking

When policies and practices fail to consider the experiences of those most impacted, organizations have lost perspective. Unfortunately, this is all too common. Decisions are made without any attempts to gain perspective.

The easiest way to solve this problem is by embedding inclusion methods in the standard practice of the organization.

Representation of any group affected by a decision or policy should be included at each stage of development, from analysis to implementation.

Leaders also benefit greatly from experiences that allow them to walk in the shoes of frontline workers. Frontline workers benefit from simulation exercises that allow them to experience the perspective of clients. Cross-training opportunities create better understanding of needs from one department to the other.

## Emotional attunement

Organizational leaders can sometimes wrongly believe they have a sense of the emotional undertones of their organizations. Worst yet, they might believe it does not matter.

Organizations can develop attunement by regularly checking the emotional state of their workforce. Although this can be accomplished through traditional surveys, there are other easier and more effective ways to get emotional feedback. Regularly employing emotional check-ins before and after meetings is one way to do this. Text or social media polls can be used to gauge an emotional reaction to changes or events without taxing the time of employees. An organization can even identify individuals to serve as the emotional barometer for specific groups.

As with individuals, emotions are often first expressed through a behavioral reaction. Increase in frequency of negative behaviors by staff or clients can be an indicator of emotional states. This can include absenteeism, outbursts, decreased productivity, or an increase in critical incidents. All of these should be viewed as an emotional distress signal. Organizations should use these signs to further explore the emotional triggers and underlying causes.

Finally, as with the individual expression of empathy, when an emotion is identified, it needs to be validated through reflection. Organizational leaders choosing to ignore obvious signs of emotional distress, convey a message that emotional experiences do not matter. This detracts from, rather than cultivates, empa-thetic expression.

# Chapter 12

# Expressing Gratitude

My introduction to developing a practice of gratitude came about twenty years ago when I received a gratitude journal as a gift from a coworker. I was inspired to commit to the practice, at least until my new journal was filled. To be honest, I think I saw it as a quick and easy way to journal more than as a method of changing my perspective. It turned out to be a bit challenging at first to come up with five things each day for which I was grateful. Soon, I found that I was paying more attention each day to things I would be able to add to my list that evening. My motivation might have been task oriented, but eventually I noticed that I became more grateful for things I used to take for granted. It got me wondering if there was something more to this gratitude thing. Beyond just the positive effects of journaling, what might be some of the other benefits of expressing gratitude?

## Change of perspective

To shift our mindset away from the unhelpful thinking of the survival brain, gratitude can be a powerful tool. Practicing gratitude can change our perception from scarcity to abundance.

In chapter six we examined some common distortions of the survival brain, including the perception of scarcity. However, the scarcity mind trap is not just a product of trauma exposure, it is consistently reinforced in the modern world. We live in a culture of not enough. We are constantly bombarded with messages telling us that we are not rich enough, thin enough, beautiful enough, or good enough. It makes it more and more difficult to see humanity in those that do not fit these worldly standards. In turn, it makes it increasingly harder to see humanity in ourselves. It is, nevertheless, still there.

Routinely practicing gratitude can begin to shift our perspective back to recognizing abundance. Among other things, an abundant mindset carries the belief that we have and we are enough. This mindset can help us battle persistent and unhelpful thoughts of shame, envy, and worry.

Additionally, because it shifts our thinking from scarcity to abundance, gratitude naturally begets generosity. Thus, increasing the likelihood of choosing a compassionate response.

## Changing our responses

In addition to promoting a perception of abundance instead of scarcity, gratitude can help us avoid another mind trap discussed in chapter six. Remember, the survival brain has a bias toward the negative. Gratitude can shift our focus from threats to solutions. This can be much more than just a mindset change. When we shift the focus away from the threat and engage the brain's ability to identify the positive, we calm the amygdala. The benefit goes beyond just helping us to self-regulate in the moment. Because of neuroplasticity, the brain can rewire our patterned responses to negative stimuli. With practice, expressing gratitude can help us to identify the positive more readily and increase our ability to self-regulate.

## Promoting general well-being

The positive effects of practicing gratitude do not stop there. There is a growing amount of research showing a link between gratitude and many aspects of well-being. This includes a strengthened immune system, reduced symptoms of illness, increased feelings of happiness, and stronger relationships.

Gratitude is also a great coping skill for dealing with anger, anxiety, or depression. We already have identified that it is a top-down strategy to calm our amygdala by shifting focus away from the threat and toward our internal or external resources. Besides that, feelings of gratitude can trigger a dopamine release. Dopamine is part of the brain's reward system so it can create a natural boost to feelings of pleasure and motivation.

## Making it a habit

Gratitude is a resiliency that can be developed over time. Like the other skill sets, it involves cultivating a habit through practice.

> **Practice Exercise:** To build a gratitude habit, try implementing one or more of the ideas below into your routine.
>
> - **Gratitude listing:** This is probably the easiest way to begin practicing gratitude. Set aside a moment each day to list at least three things for which you are thankful. This can be done as a mental exercise, but better still, write them down. The act of writing, especially putting pen or pencil to paper, can be a powerful way to encode something into our memory and, therefore, assimilate it into our perception.
>
>   This can also be a routine that you share with others. Take a few minutes each morning, during mealtime, commute, or at day's end to take turns sharing one or two things for which you are thankful.

- **Express gratitude in our relationships:** Living stressful and complex lives, it becomes easy to let the contributions of others slip from our awareness. Even if we are aware, too often we fail to simply express our appreciation. Noticing one another's efforts and simple acts of kindness takes practice. Beyond noticing, it can take deliberate intention to respond with a gesture of gratitude.

  Expressions of appreciation can be verbal or written. They do not have to be elaborate. In fact, it is more important that they are genuine and heartfelt. Start small with offering verbal acknowledgements. Try to find someone to acknowledge each day. When this becomes easier, challenge yourself to send a thank you note once a month. Remember, sometimes it just takes practice for something to become a habit.

- **Try gratitude in the face of adversity:** When life hands us a problem to solve, we often start by thinking about the difficulties of the situation. Instead, begin by thinking of the resources that will help you find a solution. Whether it is another person or your own resiliency resource, for that, you can be thankful.

  This practice sounds easy, but if we have a negative or scarcity bias, it can be a challenge in times of stress. It might be necessary to implement a cue or reminder to help you remember to shift your thinking. A cue could be as simple as a poster, meme, or sticky note. Sometimes you can use a coworker to remind you to begin with identifying resources before you get too bogged down in the situation.

When first practicing gratitude, it might be more of a cognitive or behavioral exercise. We think about what we are grateful for or we practice showing gratitude. But our thoughts, behaviors, and emotions are intertwined in the neuronal makeup of the human brain. Feeling grateful becomes the inevitable result.

Gratitude is also a cumulative resource that builds with practice. Once we label something as positive and encode it in our memory with the emotion of gratitude, it becomes easier for the brain to identify the same or similar person, object, or event as something to be thankful for the next time it is encountered.

## Organizational practices

Gratitude is more than just a shift in thinking; it is a shift in our interpersonal responses. In this way, the practice of the individual can begin to have an impact on the culture of the organization.

But organizations, too, can benefit from gratitude practices. As with individuals, expressions of gratitude do not have to be elaborate, but it is important that they are genuine and frequent.

Studies have shown that most managers think they frequently show appreciation. However, according to Wiley's study on employee motivation, the number of employees that think their managers even occasionally express appreciation is less than 20%. Too often, organizational leadership thinks they express gratitude well just because they have established a staff appreciation committee, implemented an employee of the month award, or some other practice that can sometimes be perceived as disingenuous.

It is not that these efforts are necessarily bad in themselves, but perceived lack of genuineness can dampen the intended effect. What can make a practice seem disingenuous is when it requires little thoughtful consideration on the part of management, or it is so broad that it seems like a cookie-cutter approach. This can be especially counterproductive if it coincides with decisions and policies that show a lack of appreciation for the important role of the organization's workforce. Genuine acts of appreciation are specific, individualized and reflects thoughtfulness on the part of management.

Leaders and managers play an important role in this process by taking the time to provide feedback. Too often, performance feedback is infrequent and only focused on the negative. Employees' performance also benefits from an acknowledgment of what they are doing well.

Expressing gratitude includes sharing credit for success, making sure not to overlook the role of employees at all levels in organizational accomplishments.

Most importantly, the expression of appreciation does not need to be reserved for big moments. Leaders benefit from practicing the skill of noticing everyday opportunities for appreciation. Even just doing what is expected, when requiring the amount of emotional investment human service professionals are asked to provide, deserves gratitude.

Expressions of gratitude are only the beginning. The idea is that with practice, true feelings of gratitude and appreciation become a part of the culture.

# Chapter 13

# Processing

Laura was a mid-level manager working for a state child welfare agency. Her story is probably one in which many can identify. I know I can.

Because of confidentiality, I could never really talk about the details of my job, but I did kind of talk about things in general ways. My friends and family used to love hearing about some of the crazy situations I dealt with. Then one day, my office had a case go wrong in a big way. The media ran a whole bunch of stories. It was on the news, in the papers, and everyone was talking about it. Since people knew what I did, they kept asking me what I thought. It happened everywhere I went, church, a night out with friends, and even at the grocery store. People would just come right up and ask me questions. Of course, I could not answer any of them, not even to my best friend. It was so awkward that I decided then and there to stop talking to anyone about any part of my job. Not my family or my friends.

So then, my coworkers were all I had to vent to. But all anyone ever did was complain, either about upper management or the clients. Pretty soon, it got so negative that I stopped that too. I just learned how to hold it in.

There were more bad cases, too. They didn't all make the news, but I've seen and heard some horrible things. That's a lonely place to be, having all these thoughts and images and feelings in your head and not being able to talk about it with anyone. I felt so disconnected with everyone, and I could not say a word.

Laura faced a dilemma shared by many helping professionals. We can't always talk about the work we do. Helping professionals across the human service industry choose not to share much of their work with their family and friends. If not for confidentiality reasons, they just do not want to bring the bad stuff home.

Many helping professionals I work with have found coworkers they can talk to. Although most find this helpful, like Laura, they also find conversations can quickly become negative. Too many helping professionals choose to do what Laura did and learn to "hold it in."

So why does it matter if we talk to others about what we experience? Is it because, as one helping professional described it, "When you hold all that stuff in, it feels like you will burst."? I have not come across any examples of people literally bursting, but there is evidence that putting words to our emotional experiences does help us to feel better.

I mentioned previously, that engaging our frontal cortex can calm the amygdala. It also seems that when we put a word to an emotion, a region in our prefrontal cortex is activated. This same region plays a role in emotional processing.

There might be other benefits from talking about our experiences. Communicating our experiences helps us to feel validated by another. Part of our human need for belonging involves being heard and understood. When Laura denied herself this opportunity, it left her feeling lonely and disconnected.

Even if you are not familiar with the research, I think most helping professionals intuitively know it is helpful to talk with someone about our experiences. How do we do this and maintain healthy boundaries? In Laura's story, her boundaries became blurred in several ways. First, her boundary between work and home was crossed when she was unable to separate from her work problems when she was not at work. In this case, it was both a role boundary and an information boundary, when people asked her for information she could not share. Secondly, she experienced an emotional boundary become blurred through the negativity of her coworkers. When negativity fuels negativity, venting loses its healing effect.

# Routine processing

A simple practice that can be implemented by individuals and organizations is routine processing. Routine processing is a method of acknowledging experiences that offers emotional and concrete support and allows us to let go of our work and be present for our home life.

Unprocessed events tend to cause rumination that leads to disconnection. Putting words to what is experienced helps us move away from a reactionary state, calming our stress response.

Processing should not be confused with incident inquiries, in which the purpose is to get an accurate account of a critical incident to identify the cause. Routine processing is a practice in which judging and blaming need to be suspended.

Processing can be done in a formal group setting when there has been a shared traumatic experience. Processing can also be done informally and routinely.

Individuals can develop processing routines that are a part of their daily rituals. This includes written exercises or list making at the end of the day. Writing things down is a symbolic way of releasing our thoughts. Having them on paper also gives us permission not to keep reviewing what needs to be done while we are away from work. Mental exercises can also be helpful if they include asking a set of questions to process thoughts, feelings, and events. Deep breathing can be used to symbolize the release of feelings and concerns we wish to leave at work. The commute home can be another opportunity to process if it is possible without distraction from driving.

Organizations can implement more formal procedures for processing. They can be incorporated into existing meetings and daily routines. A school administrator described the benefits of this kind of processing.

> As part of our end-of-the-day meeting, we go around the room and everyone gives one word to describe their day. It's always a little awkward for the new teachers. But I have noticed that they get better at expressing themselves once it becomes part of their routine. It also gives us all an opportunity to offer support to someone who has had a particularly negative day. I think just putting a word to the feeling helps us all to leave the day behind and start fresh in the morning.

There can also be a procedure for calling together coworkers to hold a process session on an as-needed basis. This should allow for a clarification of events and open sharing of different perspectives. This should be done in a safe and nonjudgmental environment. It might be necessary to remind participants that the purpose is to process thoughts and feelings, not to assign blame.

It is important that routine processing involves the naming of emotions. As discussed in previous chapters, labeling a difficult emotion allows us to recognize it as a temporary feeling and keeps us from overidentifying with the emotional state. Regularly acknowledging positive emotions prevents us from getting a distorted view of the world.

**Practice Exercise:** The following formats can be used to guide the process for large or small groups and can be conducted routinely or as needed.

**Group incident processing**
Situation summary (keep it brief, one person describes events and then allows clarifying questions)

*Thought reactions*
- What was your first thought or thoughts after learning of or witnessing the situation/incident?
- What was the most challenging aspect, from your perspective?

*Feelings*
- What have been some of the strongest emotions you have been experiencing?
- What body sensations did you experience?
- What are some of the losses to you or the team?

*Response*
- What was my response?

*Reflection*
- What worked well?
- Is there anything we could do differently in the future?
- What is your self-care plan, and how can you support each other moving forward?

Coworkers can also offer one-on-one processing. This can be implemented as a routine practice at the end of the day that takes no more than five to ten minutes.

*One-on-one processing*
- What was the most challenging point of the day? (What happened? What emotion did you experience? How did you respond?)
- What was the high point of today? (reflect the emotion)
- What would you like to achieve tomorrow?
- Who can support you in this goal?

Ideally, individuals have input regarding which practices work best for them.

There are many ways an organization can support this process in addition to implementing them as formal practice. They can offer training and resources to cultivate the necessary skills to both facilitate and participate. They can work to remove any identified barriers such as time and space issues. Most importantly, leaders can make room for modeling this practice in their own routine.

When organizations can implement these practices into their routines, stories like Laura's become less prevalent. Helping professionals are no longer asked to hold in their thoughts and feelings. They have an outlet to share their experiences in a way that can leave them feeling both validated and connected.

# Chapter 14
# **Connecting**

I have always been fascinated with the resiliency of rabbits. They are, in many ways, one of the most vulnerable creatures in the animal kingdom. Small and seemingly defenseless, they are prey in a world of predators.

They are also survivors. I often use them as examples to teach about human survival responses because rabbits illustrate so well how fight, flight, and freeze are used to survive. When they sense a threat, they use their strong back legs to take flight and escape harm. If there is no time for flight, they freeze. A rabbit can hold so still that they sometimes go unnoticed by would-be predators. When cornered, they also can fight. Though it is hard to imagine a vicious bunny, they will rise on their hind legs to defend themselves.

As impressive as these skills are, the thing I respect the most about rabbits is the fourth tool in their arsenal. If you have ever spent any time observing rabbits, you know that when they sense danger, they thump their hind leg. This tactic is not to scare away their predator. Rabbits are social animals. They live in underground warrens filled with more rabbits. When you see them thump, they are calling their tribe.

This illustrates perfectly, the fourth survival response. Though lesser known than fight, flight, and freeze, "connect" is arguably the most powerful survival response at our disposal.

# Benefits of connecting

As mentioned in the second chapter, the human brain has two goals. That is to survive and to thrive. Relationships are designed for both.

It is easy to see how being connected to others can increase the likelihood of survival. Since the beginning of time, human beings have been banding together to fight off predators and share resources. We now have much research evidence showing that social connectivity leads to longevity of life. In fact, isolation is as much a predictor of death as other risk factors, such as smoking, alcoholism, obesity, and lack of exercise.

But it seems our brains have always known this to be true. Just like our fight and flight response, in times of stress, our body gears up to connect by releasing a stress hormone known as oxytocin. Oxytocin fine tunes our relationship instincts, causing us to crave connection, and motivates us to seek support. It also increases empathy, causing us to be more likely to help someone else in need.

In addition to motivating us to connect, oxytocin is also produced when we connect. This neurohormone promotes well-being and stress recovery in our body. Just as there are two sides to oxytocin, social connecting can be both a survival response and a source of healing and growth.

Consider the following benefits of social connectivity:

- **Added resources:** Life's challenges require both internal and external resources to meet and overcome. Social connectivity helps to expand our external assets. This includes more than obvious tangible resources. Social connections expand our knowledge base; they offer access to new skills and they can provide a broader menu of options for solutions to problems.
- **Emotional support:** It is probably not surprising to anyone that studies show social connectivity alleviates

both depression and anxiety. Our social connections help us feel a sense of purpose and belonging that are both powerful human motivators. Whether you are experiencing good times or difficulties, it is more validating to connect with a dear friend rather than suffer alone.

- **A new mindset:** Social connections expose us to different perspectives that can challenge a stuck mindset. Seeing the world through someone else's lens can help us to let go of unhelpful beliefs such as entitlement or blaming. Recognizing the challenges that others face and even overcome makes it harder to believe that our own problems are insurmountable. Contributing solutions to problems other than our own can help us adopt mindsets of responsibility and humility. The idea that we are connected to a common humanity and that suffering is universal allows us to counteract thoughts and feelings of shame.

- **Belongingness:** We have already talked about the sense of belonging as being a basic human need. Having affiliations with social groups or support networks helps to support the feeling of belonging. Having a social support system helps us to establish emotional safety.

## Overcoming barriers to connection

So, like rabbits, we know humans are designed to connect to other humans as part of our survival response. What, then, prevents us from choosing to connect as our first response every time? The answer, I suspect, is as complicated as the human mind. Though I am no expert on rabbits, I am guessing their relationships are not nearly as complex as ours. They are probably not as burdened by past insecurities and they probably do not bring "old baggage" into new relationships.

however, rely on our past experiences to both thrive
. When our past includes relationship trauma, we can
find ourselves turning away from our greatest source
of hea__ ˍ

## Unresolved conflict

We have all probably heard that conflict can help strengthen relationships. I believe this is true, that is, if the conflict is resolved.
When unresolved, it causes pain that can quickly be labeled as a
threat by our brains. Avoiding conflict, or any early sign of conflict, can often result in avoiding connection.

## Relationship mindsets

Unresolved conflict can also reinforce stuck relationship mindsets, as discussed in chapter seven. I would like to review this
stuck mindset, which can develop when there is chronic exposure
to primary and secondary trauma.

It begins with a pervasive belief that:

- The world is unsafe
- I am unworthy of belonging
- I am uncapable of protecting myself

Because this worldview paints a reality that offers no protection, it can result in a protective mindset that believes:

- I must be in control
- My worth needs to be validated, so I can belong
- Someone else needs to be responsible

In chapter seven we also examined a mindset that can shift
our perspective and facilitate becoming unstuck:

- **Ownership:** I am responsible for my own feelings, thoughts, and behaviors (and no one else's)
- **Humility:** I am human, and all humans have flaws, and all humans have worth
- **Change:** I am not bound by my past abilities; everyone is capable of growth and change

Because of the role of perception in the interpretation function of our brains, shifting our mindset can play a powerful role in our emotional and behavioral responses. But change does not occur in thinking alone. Ultimately, it is the shift in our patterned response that creates lasting change. If we are to create connection, we need connective responses.

Ownership, humility, and change are beliefs about us. Though this mindset can facilitate connection, these beliefs should not be thought of as a response toward another. For example, it is not likely connective to attempt to make another accountable, humble, or change. Instead, the mindset of ownership, humility, and change should free us to employ a connective response such as:

- **Validation:** Affirming another's human worth and dignity
- **Forgiveness:** Letting go of past harms
- **Hope-giving:** Instilling the belief that growth is possible

Let us examine what these connective behaviors look like in practice.

## *Validation*

Validation is a response that affirms a person's inherent worth as a human being. It can include validating emotions and experiences. It also includes behaviors demonstrating respect of a person's human dignity.

Validation does not necessarily require approval of someone's behavior. It is possible to disagree with an action and still value someone as a human being. Connective responses that validate worth, recognize that as humans we all have flaws, this does not make us less human or less worthy.

Validation can simply be recognizing someone's existence. Acknowledging contributions, asking an opinion, extending an invitation, or just offering a friendly greeting are all connective responses.

Validation also recognizes that affirmation is a renewable resource that can be given with charity and generosity.

## Forgiveness

Forgiveness is about letting go of past harms. It does not mean that we continue to allow someone to violate our boundaries. It does mean that we let go of the need to seek revenge or see them be punished for a mistake or a misdeed that is in the past.

Forgiveness can open the door for restoration. But it also recognizes that the responsibility for restoration is on the one who did the harm. The responsibility for healing is on the one who has been harmed.

## Hope-giving

Hope-giving responses are connective responses that instill the belief that growth and change are possible. Hope-giving responses include acknowledging improvement and small increments of change. It celebrates victories no matter the size.

Hope-giving can also include using language that focuses on solutions and conveys that their problems can be overcome. It uses words like "yet," as in "you haven't learned that yet," to demonstrate that people are not limited to their current skill set.

All these connective responses deepen the quality of relationships. In that way, they benefit the giver and the receiver.

# Social connectivity

The benefit of connecting is not limited to close relationships. Social connecting can include coworkers, shared interest groups, or the people with whom you share your daily commute. Of course, social connectivity is about more than just having 1,000-plus Facebook friends. Social connectivity is about quality relationships and meaningful community interactions.

**Practice Exercise:** There are many ways to increase our social connectivity and cultivate this important resiliency. Choose one or more of the following ideas to try.

1. Go to lunch with a friend.
2. Host a neighborhood porch party.
3. Participate in a walk-a-thon or some other fundraising event.
4. Join a book club or start a movie club.
5. Volunteer! Either call a local organization or sign up for a volunteer match program online.
6. Schedule a reoccurring fun activity like game night or a potluck dinner with close friends or family.
7. Pick up a new hobby and invite others to join you or find a group that already exists.
8. Phone a friend or relative that you have not talked to in a while.
9. Invite someone to attend a community or cultural event with you.
10. Make it a point to smile and greet the people you encounter each day.

There are many other ways you might think of to boost your opportunities to connect. Share with your coworkers and exchange ideas to grow this list.

# Organizational connecting

Organizations also benefit from practices that both facilitate opportunities to connect for their workforce and model connective responses. Employees who are reaping the benefits of connecting are happier and healthier. A happier and healthier workforce helps create an environment that is not only more productive but is more conducive to compassionate responses.

## Facilitate connection

Organizations can either encourage or discourage their employees to connect in meaningful ways. Here are some practices that encourage connection:

- **Group supervision and peer consultation:** Most organizations view supervision as a linear and hierarchical function. Often industry or accreditation standards require this traditional method of supervision. Though, even when this is the case, an organization can still benefit from utilizing groups to provide consultation. This process broadens the support resources available to the individual. Just as important, team members learn the strengths and needs of their coworkers. This facilitates reciprocal support that is a foundation for building relationship.
- **Create space:** Environment drives practice. Private offices and high-walled cubicles can create the necessary physical boundaries for task completion. However, this environment alone provides little opportunity for interaction. Home-based workforces create an even greater challenge. Therefore, having spaces available where people can interact regularly during the workday is crucial. Keep in mind, if the only place coworkers can interact is the break room, the organization is sending

the message that cultivating connection is something you need to do on your own time. The goal here is to value connection as part of the work we do.

- **Share celebrations:** High-point events are opportunities to connect. Making it a habit to celebrate them, especially over food, brings people together. High points can be birthdays, work anniversaries, promotions, or anything else worth celebrating. With work that is often focused on negative events, it is important to create opportunity to connect over positive events.

- **Group projects:** Encourage opportunities for collaboration on work-related projects both departmentally and across various work groups. Sharing ideas, successes, and failures helps people to learn from each other. Presenting regular opportunities to work together cultivates the strengths of the whole team. It also provides opportunity for connection both to individuals and to the group.

- **Team building:** Team building is about creating opportunities to identify with a group in a positive way. Most team-building exercises are centered around group goals or task completion, but they do not have to be work related. Friendly competitions or group challenges can include anything from weight loss to trivia games. Most importantly, they create the feeling of being connected and belonging to the group.

- **Provide networking opportunities outside the organization:** Connection does not just have to occur within the organization. Helping professionals also benefit from feeling connected to the larger system and community. When organizations provide these opportunities within the context of the work week, they demonstrate that this is a priority. Networking events can include training, conferences, community service events, community-wide work groups, or professional affiliations. The benefit is not just connection for the individual, but it creates connections for the organization.

## Practice connective responses

As previously discussed, connective responses include validation, forgiveness, and hope-giving. That is, these are the responses that provide a different experience to those that have experienced relationship trauma. In an organization, when connective responses are embedded in practice at all levels, they become part of a culture of compassion.

An organization that practices validation routinely acknowledges the needs, emotions, experiences, and opinions of their employees. This acknowledgement is demonstrated not just in seeking information but in the response to the information. Leaders model the act of sharing credit and acknowledging the contribution of others.

An organization that practices forgiveness provides an environment where people are not afraid to make mistakes. Procedures support their ability to safely do their job so that mitigated mistakes can be a part of the learning process. Leaders view setbacks as an opportunity for improvement. Instead of looking for someone to pin the blame on, they look to identify systemic problems that can be adjusted to ensure better outcomes.

An organization that practices hope-giving provides opportunities for their workforce to learn and grow. Leaders focus on strengths and potential skill areas to develop instead of seeing people as being fixed in their abilities. Performance evaluations are used to create opportunities for both the individual and the organization to work toward a shared goal, not just to highlight failures and weed out underperformers.

## Establish a process for resolving conflict

Conflict is an inevitable part of human interaction. As mentioned previously, unresolved conflict can create disconnection.

So it makes sense that organizations that develop processes to resolve conflict increase the opportunities for positive relationships among their employees.

Conflict resolution is a high-level skill that even professionals in the field of human service can struggle with. More accurately, conflict resolution is a complex skill set that requires many skills, including self-awareness, perspective taking, feelings identification, listening, communicating needs, and self-regulation.

Most conflicts involve a perceived threat, and it is our brain's response to the perceived threat that perpetuates the conflict. Utilizing tools such as the reenactment triangle introduced in chapters' seven and ten can help provide awareness of unhelpful responses. Though, often it can be difficult for individuals to come to this level of self-awareness. Organizations can support self-awareness by providing training and regular use of the triangle in supervision and consultations.

But individuals who have been triggered by a perceived threat of a conflict might need further assistance to achieve resolution. Having a process led by a trained facilitator can help organizations and individuals to address conflict to create a better relationship outcome.

There are many conflict-resolution models that organizations can choose from. Helpful models have many things in common. All create an opportunity to identify the varying perspectives of the individuals or groups involved in the conflict. They acknowledge a distinction between emotions and perception and the role they play in how individuals view the problem. This allows participants to find a common ground to move toward in resolution. Resolution involves individuals or groups identifying their needs and what they are willing to do.

**Practice Exercise:** The following is an example of a conflict-resolution process that can be used with the worksheet provided at the end of this chapter:

1. Begin by setting any ground rules anyone needs to feel safe in this process. The facilitator can begin by offering suggestions such as listen without interruption while the other is speaking. Everyone has a right to their emotions and perceptions, etc.

2. Allow each person or group to identify the emotions involved for them in this conflict. Each person or group should have an opportunity to speak uninterrupted. Instruct each to listen while the other person is sharing how they feel. The emotions are recorded in the boxes labeled "Emotion." Each of the opposing viewpoints has its own box. (If the conflict is between two individuals, the facilitator can choose to have each reflect what they heard.)

3. Next, each person or group shares their perspective one at a time without interruption. Again, the other person is instructed to listen. Each side can clarify any misperceptions when it is their turn.

4. In the center box, record the points that everyone agreed on. The facilitator can offer suggestions to get them started.

5. Each person or group takes turns identifying what they need in relation to the conflict.

6. Each person or group takes turns offering what they are willing to do in response to the other's needs.

7. As a point of agreement is reached, it can be recorded in the center box.

8. Conclude the process with a quick emotion word check-in to describe how the participants felt about the process. Restate what each is willing to do and offer follow-up, as necessary.

This method can be used for resolving conflict between two individuals or two groups. Keep in mind that this skill can be introduced in a formal training, but it improves with practice. Organizations should not wait for major conflicts to utilize these practices. The above process or similar processes should be practiced routinely with the goal of both elevating the conflict resolution skills of all the employees and resolving conflicts while they are still manageable.

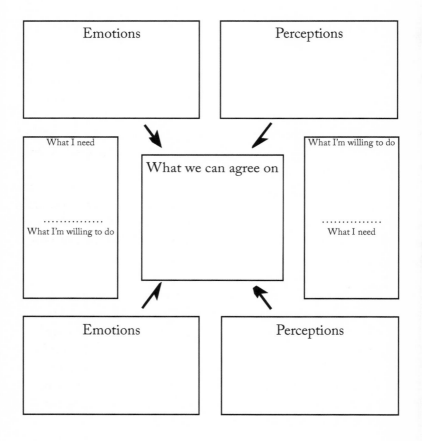

# Chapter 15
# Planning for Self-Care

Those who have flown have no doubt heard the flight attendants instruct us that in the case of an emergency we should secure our oxygen masks before attempting to assist others. As counterintuitive as this may sound to those who routinely put the needs of others before their own, it is not callous or selfish. It is simply the logical recognition that without oxygen, we can be of no help to anyone.

Yet, for helping professionals to accept this logic, we must overcome barriers in our work environment, job demands, and even our own mind traps that keep us from making self-care a priority. Shawna, a therapist I interviewed, illustrated this point well in her story:

> It is so important to be there for my clients, but on days when I have back-to-back sessions, it can be so draining. When I start to feel this way, I tell myself "just suck it up" and keep going. After all, this is what I wanted to do. But I find that I am losing the joy that made me want to do this work in the first place. I want to be able to enjoy my job, but I am giving so much of myself at work that at the end of the day, there is nothing left for me.
>
> Like, I promised myself that I would spend my weekends reading more, something I used to enjoy. But when the weekend rolls around, I am too exhausted to think.
>
> To be honest, it is not just the job that makes self-care for me so difficult. I think it is so a part of my nature to help and to give that it has become my identity. I have

started recognizing that sometimes I feel that if I am not a giver, I must be a taker and that doesn't sit well with me. I know this is extreme thinking, but it is there, and it causes me to stretch my limits and avoid making giving myself time a priority.

Prioritizing self-care means acknowledging that you need care. One of the problems I have is the unrealistic expectation that everyone seems to have of me. It's like as therapists, we can't be broken. This happens at work and at home. The other day I was talking to my mother about a family disagreement when she said to me, "Well, you should be able to deal with this better, you are a therapist." I just lost it. I actually yelled into the phone, "I'm allowed to struggle, too."

Indeed, prioritizing self-care requires acknowledging that we, too, can be broken. The fact that we are broken, drained, exhausted, or struggling serves as a reminder of our humanness. Helping professionals are humans who have needs that need tending, so we can replenish the abundance of compassion we all possess.

## Numbing is not self-care

Taking care of oneself is an essential element in combating compassion fatigue and cultivating compassion. Those who suffer from chronic exposure to stress and secondary trauma are left exhausted and can feel a need to shut out the source of their pain. Unfortunately, this leads some to choose activities in the name of "self-care" that involve numbing our emotional connections. This can create a disconnect when what we need is to reconnect.

I am not just referring to drinking or other substance use. Numbing can also include "vegging" in front of the television, boredom eating, playing repetitive games on your phone, or mindlessly scrolling through social media. None of these activities are necessarily harmful in themselves. They just might lack the nourishing connection that real self-care can provide. Even worse, it is difficult to selectively numb negative emotions without losing the positive ones. Thus, we are inadvertently denying ourselves the source of genuine healing and revitalization.

There is a valid need to transition from work to home, but this should involve identifying feelings not numbing them. As noted in a previous chapter, it is useful to develop habits to help process the events and emotions of the day. Transition rituals, like routine processing, create a healthy boundary that allows us to put the day behind us and be present for other aspects of our life.

Additionally, we all occasionally need to unwind from a challenging day's work, especially those who work in stressful environments. However, there is a fine line between what is relaxing and what is numbing. When we are effectively caring for our mind, body, and spirit, we should feel a sense of rejuvenation. Remember, it is not the activity itself that is the problem; it is how you are engaging in it. It is up to you to determine if you are engaging in an activity to numb or to connect.

**Reflective Exercise:** When choosing to unwind, ask yourself the following questions:

- Does this activity help me to feel rejuvenated?
- Does this activity help me to focus?
- Does this activity increase my awareness?
- Can I keep track of time during this activity, as opposed to time slipping away without my knowledge?
- Does this activity help me to sleep better?

Try to choose activities that you can answer yes to.

The slipping away of time can be an indicator that we are numbing our sense of awareness. However, it should be noted that there are some activities that cause us to be unaware of time that are not necessarily numbing. An example of this would be the concept of "flow." Flow is often described by athletes, and rock climbers as "being in the zone," or completely absorbed in an activity just for the sake of the activity. For those of you who are not rock climbers, you may have experienced a zone of productivity where you are so focused on your work that the day goes by fast, but a lot is accomplished. I am sure we have all experienced a pleasurable day in which we remark with the adage "time flies when you're having fun." However, in all these examples, the memory of the experience is complete and full. This is quite different than a numbing experience where there is little to account for the time spent.

## Choosing self-care

Of course, effective self-care involves developing habits that incorporate self-care strategies into our regular routines. It is a deliberate choice to engage in activities that are restorative. Another way of thinking of it is that self-care is being compassionate with ourselves. It goes beyond just acknowledging that we have needs; it requires us to respond, not retreat, in proactive ways.

Here are just a few self-care ideas that are connective:

- **Engaging the senses:** Activities that engage our senses ground us to the present. This might include listening to music, appreciating visual art, noticing beauty in nature, getting a massage, or savoring a nutritious meal. Enlivening the five senses of touch, sound, sight, smell, and taste, heighten our awareness as well as our appreciation of our surroundings.
- **Rest and relaxation:** Ensuring a good night's sleep is

one of the most compassionate things we can do for both our bodies and our minds. In addition to committing to a reasonable bedtime, it is also important to learn relaxation techniques that incorporate body awareness. Techniques like deep breathing, progressive muscle relaxation and meditation help us to switch on our parasympathetic nervous system to decompress from our stress responses and increase our body's ability to rest.

- **Taking walks:** We all know exercising is good for the body, but it does not have to involve going to the gym. Just get moving. A walk around the block can help you process your thoughts, fill your lungs with fresh air, and circulate your blood. Doing it outdoors gives you the added benefit of connecting with nature.

- **Nourishing the body:** Our body needs water and nutrients to grow and heal. So just taking the time to simply drink water or mindfully chose to eat something nutritious is an act of self-compassion. Aside from the obvious health benefits, it feels good to know you are giving your body what it needs.

- **Feeding the soul:** Activities that help us find meaning and connection to something greater than ourselves nurtures our spiritual well-being. This can include prayer, worship, inspirational reading, music, service, or fellowship with those who share your beliefs.

- **Being creative:** Write, sing, craft, cook, paint, build, sew, dance, act ... there are an endless number of ways you can choose to be creative. Being creative in any form involves emotional expression at some level. Creativity can reduce stress and increase your ability to problem solve. Besides, there is no denying the surge of positive energy that comes from creating something.

- **Recreation and leisure:** I like to lead participants in my self-care trainings in an exercise that involves naming the activities that they did as a child or young adult that brought them joy. So often we push play or other amusements out of our lives because we view it as unimportant. When in fact, they can be a valuable contribution to our overall well-being.

Exploring new areas of interest can lead to new opportunities for learning and enjoyment. Recreation and leisure activities can be engaged in solitude or with others, at home or in our community. It is about discovering ways to provide enrichment in your life outside of work.

> **Reflective Exercise:** Adding recreational activities does not always require finding new things to do. Sometimes we just need to rediscover what used to bring us joy. Try answering the following questions and see if you can identify something you would like to add, reintroduce, or do more of in your life.
>
> - What brings you joy?
> - What activities do you enjoy doing?
> - When were you the happiest? What did you do then?
> - What would you do if you had a day to yourself?
> - What were your favorite activities as a child?
> - What hobbies do you enjoy? (past or present)
> - What new things would you like to try or learn?

Though choosing effective self-care strategies like those mentioned above might involve a little more thought and planning, there is an added benefit. Practicing self-care that is connective instead of numbing can increase our ability to connect with others, and as we have already established, social connectivity is one of our most powerful sources of healing and resiliency.

It is important to note that proper self-care is a deliberate and preventative action. It is not a reactionary measure to be taken when we are at the end of our rope. Instead, it is a practice that is woven into our daily, weekly, and monthly routines. For some, rejuvenating activities are already a scheduled priority. Too often, this is not the case for helping professionals. Their scheduled lives are full of caring for others at the expense of their own well-being. Mind traps support the notions that there is not enough time, and our own care should not be a priority. This creates a negative cycle of resentfulness and shame that ironically can diminish our ability to truly be there for others in the way we desire.

Therefore, we must remind ourselves of the logic behind the flight attendant's instructions to secure our oxygen first. It takes courage to put on the mask so you can be at your best when you are needed.

## Organizational self-care

So, what does it look like when an organization is practicing self-care?

As with individuals, self-care is a deliberate and proactive choice. It comes with the recognition that caring for the culture and well-being of the organization is in the best interest of its employees and the people they serve.

This involves the ability to make value-based decisions, as mentioned in chapter five.

I have witnessed organizations make reactionary decisions that might divert a short-term crisis, but it comes at the expense of their long-term well-being.

Proactivity also means overcoming mind traps that do not allow for the investment in ventures that will help the organization to thrive.

## Facilitating employee self-care

In the human service arena, organizations are getting better at recognizing the need to encourage self-care for their employees.

Unfortunately, I think they sometimes struggle with how to effectively support it.

Even worse, sometimes organizations unwittingly set up barriers to practicing self-care. Therefore, the first step needs to be identifying and removing those obstacles. One of the greatest barriers for an organization to overcome is the underlying message that employee self-care is something to do after all the work is done. The problem with this message is that in the human service field, the work is never done. Self-care then, needs to be woven into our routine both at work as well as at home.

Self-care is a skill set, and one that needs to be cultivated. Opportunities for skill development in this area can include formal training. Training can focus on recognizing the need for self-care, expanding ideas, and teaching specific skills. But self-care skills are also strengthened with practice. There are many opportunities organizations can provide to facilitate practicing employee self-care. The following list offers some suggestions.

- **Morning stretch:** Providing a space where employees can meet for a group-led stretch and exercise routine is a great way to start the day.
- **Mindfulness minutes:** These can be short breaks (one to ten minutes) throughout the day to encourage the practice of simple mindfulness techniques.
- **Reading hours:** Reading, whether it is directly or indirectly related to work, is so important to our continued learning and growth. Yet rarely do organizations allow time for even professional reading. Reading hours or half-hours are established times where employees have permission to just read (or listen to a podcast.) Discussion groups or professional book clubs add to the benefit.
- **Walking groups:** If your organization is lucky enough to be located on grounds or in a neighborhood good for walking, find ways to encourage employees to take advantage of the opportunity to walk.

- **Creativity breaks:** Allow break rooms to offer opportunities to exercise creativity through art activities, cooking, crafts, brainstorming sessions, or many other activities that boost creativity. These types of breaks can be short, simple, and employee led.
- **Nutritional options:** This does not mean policing habits or pulling every sugary snack out of the vending machines. It simply means offering healthy options for people trying to practice healthy eating.
- **Good health challenges:** A fun way to encourage healthy choices is through friendly competitions, like a healthy recipe contest or a walk-a-thon, which supports and values positive change.
- **Recreational opportunities:** Company softball teams, trivia competitions, and theater nights are just a few possibilities. Recreational opportunities could be as simple as board games in the lunchroom.

Ironically, many of the above ideas have been practiced in successful corporations in other industries for years.

## Self-care plans

Self-care plans are another popular way to facilitate employee self-care. These are proactive plans developed by individuals committed to routinely practicing self-care. I've seen organizations successfully implement self-care plans. They have taken the following approaches:

- **Turn shame into solidarity:** Although self-care plans are the responsibility of the individual, making it a shared practice helps to alleviate any shame surrounding making your own care a priority. When it is the expectation for everyone from the senior executive to the frontline and behind-the-scenes employees, it instead becomes something that can cultivate a sense of belonging. It also creates opportunities for positive peer pressure and encouragement.

- **Offer a template:** Though the plans themselves need to be individualized, it helps to offer a uniform template for creating a self-care plan. There are a variety of templates available. Good ones acknowledge that self-care touches many domains of life, such as physical, psychological, spiritual, emotional, social, and professional. Additionally, a good self-care plan offers ideas that should be practiced daily, weekly, or monthly. You want the chosen template to acknowledge this.
- **Use them in supervision:** Organizations should avoid the mistake of encouraging employees to develop a self-care plan and then never mentioning it again. They are meant to be used. Self-care plans are great coaching tools. They can be a resource to build a necessary skill set to deal with the demands of the job. A self-care plan is also a living document that can evolve and change as the individual does. New ideas can be added, and outdated ones removed.

*Caveat: Though self-care plans have many positive uses in an organization, be careful they are not used for coercion, manipulation, shaming, or any other tactic that draws people into the unhealthy relationship patterns and reenactments discussed in previous chapters.*

# Conclusion

As human service professionals, we cannot seek to repair our communities without first seeking to repair ourselves. This begins with the restoration of compassion to the fatigued.

Compassion is not like a cup that is either empty or full. Compassion is a renewable resource generated through our interconnectedness. For helping professionals, restoring compassion requires seeing ourselves as recipients, not just dispensers of compassion. We are like a conduit through which compassion flows.

Restoring the flow of compassion to our organizations is a journey, but do not make the mistake of seeing it as a journey with an end. Until we live in a world without suffering, cultivating compassion is an ongoing process. This process begins with self-awareness and regulation, but it also includes an on-going commitment to develop and practice the skill sets and mindsets that cultivate compassion.

So what would it look like if our organizations flowed abundantly with compassion?

What would it feel like to be thriving instead of just surviving?

What if the culture of our organizations were that of compassion, not just for others but for each other?

In addition to compassionate responses and the regular practice of the skill sets addressed in Part III, here are some other signs that an organization has moved away from survival mode and is thriving.

- **Accountability:** Both leaders and employees step up to take responsibility for their part when things go wrong so that solutions can be sought. The organization encourages accountability through clear expectations, learning opportunities, and choice.

- **Empowerment:** The organization develops and inspires employees at all levels, demonstrating that all people have the potential for growth and change. Employees and service community have a voice in the decisions they are impacted by.
- **Awareness:** Leaders and employees have an accurate perception of the challenges their organization might face.
- **Ownership:** All employees and members of the service community have a sense of shared ownership in outcomes of the work. Support for each other is freely given.
- **Abundance:** Programs and employees have the resources they need to be successful.
- **Conflict resolution:** Conflicts are viewed as learning opportunities and addressed in a timely manner.
- **Sense of safety:** Employees and the service community feel safe in the knowledge that they will be treated fairly. This includes being safe to express opinions and perceptions that differ from leadership.
- **Emotional expression:** There are healthy avenues for emotional expression.
- **Attunement:** Leaders and employees are attuned to the emotional pulse of the organization and service community.
- **Responsible decision-making:** Decisions are guided by agency values, future expectations, and those most impacted by the decision.
- **Transparency:** Information flow is bidirectional, clear, and open. Leadership is open to learning from all members of the organization and service community. Regular feedback is encouraged and sought.
- **Innovation:** Questioning and experimentation within the scope of the organization's mission and values is encouraged. Both success and failures are embraced as learning opportunities.

- **Integrity:** Practices accurately reflect agency values.
- **Purpose:** There is a clear connection between the work being done and the mission of the organization.

Though this book primarily focuses on helping professionals in human service organizations, the need for combating compassion fatigue extends beyond the social service world. I have heard from individuals in other sectors who tell me they, too, have experienced similar symptoms when exposed to secondary trauma.

I read an article about Uber that points to this very thing. Uber became aware that their special investigative unit was beginning to suffer the impact of investigating everything from assaults and threats to other traumatic incidents. Faced with the effects of secondary trauma, the company had to rethink the way they provided support to their employees working in this capacity.

This is just one example of a mainstream company that has employees impacted by compassion fatigue. If you are dealing with people, you are going to have to acknowledge the impact of trauma. It is time we recognize that violence and trauma have an impact on all of us. Even witnessing trauma secondhand can create a ripple effect that takes its toll on our families and communities.

I hope this book will be a call to action for the human service community to lead the way.

In the introduction of this book I offered a challenge. I challenged you to embrace your humanity with vulnerability and at the same time own your ability to be an agent of change. I also asked that you remain hopeful. Because when we recognize that organizational culture reflects human interaction, we realize the power we each possess to change the trajectory.

As individuals, we can all commit to self-awareness and regulation. Together, we can sharpen the skills of establishing boundaries, exercising empathy, processing, expressing gratitude, connecting, and planning for self-care. We can embed these habits into our work and as reflected in our interactions with each other. We can embody compassion for ourselves and our communities.

The ideas expressed in this book are based on my experience as well as a growing body of research on the human brain and the power of compassion. But this is just the beginning. More research is needed, and we all need to continue learning from what is discovered. Brave individuals and organizations need to see this as a challenge to explore the solutions, continue doing what works well, and spread the hope that compassion is not and never will be depleted.

# Notes

## Introduction

ProQOL is a self-assessment designed to measure compassion satisfaction and compassion fatigue.

Stories: To prepare for this book and in my work with human service organizations, I have interviewed and listened to the stories of dozens of human service professionals. The stories I have included reflect those first-hand accounts. To maintain anonymity for the individuals and organizations they work for, I have removed identifying details, paraphrased, and in some cases, combined elements of more than one story.

## Chapter 1: Call for Action

Van Mol, M. M., Kompanje, E. J., Benoit, D. D., Bakker, J., & Nijkamp, M. D. (2015). The prevalence of compassion fatigue and burnout among healthcare professionals in intensive care units: A Systematic Review. *PLOS ONE*, 10(8). Retrieved September 4, 2020, from https://doi.org/10.1371/journal.pone.0136955.

Ginnivan, L. (2014). The dirty history of doctors' hands, *Method Quarterly*. Retrieved September 4, 2020, from http://www.methodquarterly.com/2014/11/handwashing/.

Joinson, C. (1992) Coping with compassion fatigue, *Nursing 92*: 22(4), 116, 118–119, 121.

Felliti, V. J., et al. (1998). Relationship of childhood abuse and household dysfunction to many of the leading causes of death in adults. The Adverse Childhood Experiences (ACE) Study. *American Journal of Preventative Medicine, 14*, 245–258.

Figley, C.R. (Ed.) (1995). *Compassion fatigue: secondary traumatic stress disorders from treating the traumatized.* New York, Brunner/Mazel.

## Chapter 2: The Brain

Wallisch, P. (2017). Illumination assumptions account for individual differences in the perceptual interpretation of a profoundly ambiguous stimulus in the color domain: the dress. *Journal of Vision*, 17(5).

## Chapter 3: Secondary Trauma and Compassion Fatigue

Stanford University has a department dedicated to research on compassion and altruism. Their website and research can be found at http://ccare.stanford.edu/.

Filkowski MM, Cochran RN, Haas BW. (2016) Altruistic behavior: mapping responses in the brain. *Neuroscience and Neuroeconomics*, 5, 65–75. Retrieved September 4, 2020, from https://doi.org/10.2147/NAN.S87718.

Weng, H.Y., Lapate, R.C ., Stodola, D. E., Rogers, G.M., Davidson, R.J. (2018) Visual attention to suffering after compassion training is associated with decreased amygdala responses. *Frontiers in Psychology*, 9. Retrieved September 4, 2020, from 10.3389/fpsyg.2018.00771.

# Chapter 4: Body Responses

I recommend the following two books for more information on body responses and regulation:

Van der Kolk, Bessel A. (2014). *The Body Keeps the Score: Brain, Mind, and Body in the Healing of Trauma.* New York, Viking.

Dana, Deb (2018) *Polyvagal Theory in Therapy: Engaging the Rhythm of Regulation.* New York, W.W. Norton and Company.

# Chapter 5: Emotional Responses

Ryan, R. M., & Deci, E. L. (2000). Self-determination theory and the facilitation of intrinsic motivation, social development, and well-being. *American Psychologist*, 55(1), 68–78.

# Chapter 6: Cognitive Responses

Stetson, C., Fiesta, M.P., Eagleman, D.M. (2007) Does time really slow down during a frightening event? *PLOS ONE* 2(12). Retrieved September 4, 2020, from https://doi .org/10.1371/journal.pone.0001295.

Findings from The Philadelphia Urban Ace Survey. (2013) Prepared by The Research and Evaluation Group at Public Health Management Corporation, Philadelphia.

Esaki, N., & Larkin, H. (2013). Prevalence of adverse childhood experiences (ACEs) among child service providers. Families in Society: The Journal of Contemporary Social Services, 94(1), 31–37.

Van der Kolk, B. (1989) The compulsion to repeat the trauma: Reenactment, revictimization, and masochism. *Psychiatric Clinics of North America*, 12, 389–411.

# Chapter 7: Relationship Responses

Karpman, S. (1968). Fairy tales and script drama analysis. *Transactional Analysis Bulletin*, 7(26), 39–43.

The idea of the persecutor, rescuer, and victim roles being expressions of our fight, flight and freeze response was first introduced to me by my colleague Lesa Chandler when we were co-presenting at a conference in June of 2017.

# Chapter 11: Exercising Empathy

Winnerman, Lea (2005) The Mind's Mirror, American Psychological Association's *Monitor on Psychology* (Vol 38 No 9 page 48).

Decety, J., & Moriguchi, Y. (2007). The empathic brain and its dysfunction in psychiatric populations: implications for intervention across different clinical conditions, *Biopsychosocial Med.*, 1(22).

# Chapter 12: Expressing Gratitude

The Greater Good Science Center at the University of California, Berkeley's Expanding the Science and Practice of Gratitude Project. Retrieved September 4, 2020, from http://greatergood.berkeley.edu/expandinggratitude.

Wiley, C. (1997). What motivates employees according to over 40 years of motivation surveys, *International Journal of Manpower*, 18(3), 263–280.

## Chapter 13: Processing

University of California, Los Angeles. (2007). Putting feelings into words produces therapeutic effects in the brain. *ScienceDaily*. Retrieved September 4, 2020, from www.sciencedaily.com/releases/2007/06/070622090727.htm.

## Chapter 14: Connecting

House, J.S., Landis, K.R., Umberson, D. (1988). *Science*, 241(4865), 540–545. Retrieved September 4, 2020, from 10.1126/science.3399889.

Wu, Jade Ph.D. (2020) The Power of Oxytocin, *Psychology Today*. Retrieved September 4, 2020, from www.psychologytoday.com/us/blog/the-savvy-psychologist/202002/the-power-oxytocin.

## Conclusion

O'Brien, S.A., Black, N., Griffin, D., Stressed out and at risk: Inside Uber's special investigation unit, CNN Business, January 21, 2019.

# Acknowledgements

I would like to acknowledge all my colleagues who allowed me to share my ideas and who offered feedback. I have learned from all of you. A special thanks to Connie, Shannon, Traci, Amy, Jim, Judi, Sheila, and Pam. Your wisdom and encouragement kept me moving forward.

I am grateful for the group of professionals who assisted me in turning my ideas into a book. Shana Murph, my editor, helped me shape my words and sharpen my message. Your insight was invaluable. My designer, Kelsey Klockenteger, made it look polished.

I am blessed to come from a large supportive family including a sister who is always available for technical or creative assistance.

Lastly, this book would not have been possible without the many helping professionals who have graciously opened their hearts and shared their stories. Your compassion continues to inspire me.

# About the Author

Michelle Graff is the founder of Cultivating Human Resiliency and the author of *The Compassion Fatigued Organization*. After more than twenty years in social services, she now focuses on helping the helping professional.

As a resiliency cultivator, she provides training and consultation to both public and private human service agencies. Over the past twenty-two years, Michelle has developed and presented hundreds of trainings on everything from trauma and the brain to interpersonal and leadership skills. Her experience working with human service professionals and organizations has provided an insider's perspective on the impact of secondary trauma. Compassion fatigue has become her most requested topic.

Michelle lives and works in Kansas City, where she enjoys learning, creating, and spending time with family and friends.

Made in the USA
Middletown, DE
19 April 2023

29099636R00094